Ill Thoughts, Ill Words, Ill Deeds

Ill Thoughts, Ill Words, Ill Deeds

A Toxick Magick Primer: Volume 1

Joshua Wetzel

Megalithica Books
Stafford, England

Cover Artwork: Danielle Lainton
Editors: Derrick Penrod & Danielle Lainton
Layout: Danielle Lainton

Set in Book Antiqua

MB0213
ISBN: 978-1-912241-21-7
A Megalithica Books Publication
http://www.immanion-press.com
info@immanion-press.com

Table of Contents

Foreword

Throughout history, people have engaged in practical magick to exert control over themselves, others, and the environment. The modern age is no exception. Just like in antiquity, magick provides a means to acquire health, wealth, fame, love, and more. It provides power to the powerless.

Ill Thoughts, Ill Words, Ill Deeds comes to us at a critical time. Today, many people feel they lack control over their lives. Some are unsure how to regain control, while others never had any in the first place. Toxick magick provides a means to reclaim this control. In addition to elucidating key concepts and principles of magick in a refreshing, accessible manner, *Ill Thoughts, Ill Words, Ill Deeds* provides effective exercises that are valuable for novices and experienced practitioners alike.

If you are willing to put in the work, you can change yourself and your universe. Josh will show you the way. He is one of the most talented, innovative magicians I know. He also has loads of common sense. Doing magick with him is always a blast! Relax – you are in good hands.

Soror Velchanes
author of *The Elemental Magic Workbork*

Introduction

Many years ago, not long after I had first become interested in chaos magick, Christopher Hyatt released "The Toxick Magician". As someone who was always fascinated by what is commonly referred to as the "Left Hand Path" schools of magick, I eagerly acquired a copy of Hyatt's new work the moment it was available. To this day number 88 of the original pressing of 100 sits on one of my shelves. However, I must confess, it did not live up to my expectations. While Satanism and it's offshoot Setianism, Chaos Magick, Thelema, and other LHP approaches to the occult provided viable frameworks to construct rituals, design experiments, and formulate new theories and techniques..." The Toxick Magician" failed to do so.

Even when it was expanded later into "The Psychopath's Bible," the core of a system for doing magick was woefully absent. It felt like a stillbirth. It was, to me, a philosophical perspective without the underlying machinery to turn thought into action. Worse, both carried a finality about them. Toxick magick began and ended with those two efforts. Like GMO[1] seeds that produce only a single yield, "The Toxick Magician" and "The Psychopath's Bible" were ultimately sterile.

It seemed then to me, as it does now, like a missed opportunity. Chaos magick gave range to a limitless number of possible permutations. It was (and is) a metaparadigmal approach to doing magick that can be overlayed on an existing magical system (to render it effective) or used as the base to design a new system. Chaos magick, I thought, was moreover headed in the

---

[1] Genetically Modified Organism

right direction. It could, in theory, allow the magician to drop all the baggage—both spiritual and linguistic—that clung to earlier approaches. I was left dumbfounded that toxick magick didn't pick up where Peter Carroll, Phil Hine, Dave Lee, Nicholas Hall, and others left off.

What opportunity was missed? Nothing less than the creation of a magical system focused entirely on the magician and the ability of their mind to be used as the ultimate tool to shape the reality they experience. A manifestation, moreover, with a purpose: the corruption of reality; the poisoning of centuries-old religious, political, and spiritual orthodoxy; the magician as the main agent of disruption, the results of which rebound to their benefit and the benefit of all.

With that said, the following pages will lay out the philosophy and techniques of toxick magick. It is my sincere hope that it will provide a framework for the practitioner's future growth and success. I believe that with determination, persistence, and the right methodology[2], just about anything is possible. All that is required is the will to do the work. The desired results will inevitably follow. Shall we get started?

---

[2] Not to mention a lack of squeamishness.

Chapter 1
Journaling (observation of self and use of time and habits)

In order to use magick effectively to reach one's goals a practitioner needs to understand the point from which they start. That sentiment may seem cliche to the point of one asking: "So why even bring it up?" I would say the answer comes in several parts. Firstly, I feel that if there is one thing we as human beings are exceptionally good at it's lying to ourselves, like a two year old thinking that if they can't see something then it can't see them. If we can't see our own shortcomings and limitations they must not exist. If our negative habits don't exist, we don't have to address them. The result is a state of feeling that what we have now is "good enough" - when it often is not. Secondly, on perhaps the other end of the scale, people readily dismiss or overlook aptitudes and talents, dismissing them as "no big deal" - not realizing that they are valuable tools that can be brought to bear to engineer success.[3]

Exercise 1: Aptitudes and Aggravations

In pursuit of this, we first need to come up with a list about ourselves. What are my strengths? What are my weaknesses? What are my good habits? What are my bad habits? Obviously no two lists will look alike and frankly, no list will be 100% symmetrical between good and bad. You can start this list yourself, but I also recommend reaching out to friends and family to get as well rounded a picture of yourself as possible. Sometimes those near to

---

[3] Success in the most basic sense equates to getting what you want.
Failure — not getting what you want.

us see things in us that we miss: good and bad. Their observations are worth taking into account. It's easy enough to get their feedback, too. Heck, you can even throw it out on social media, "Hey everyone, I'm just curious, what do you think are the three best things about me?" Or "Hey everyone, is there anything I do or have done that you thought was shit? I'm trying to work on myself a bit for <insert reason here>."

Once you have that list, keep it as the first page of your journal. Here is an example of my own:

My List

Aptitudes	Aggravations
Creative	Procrastinates
Intelligent	Lazy
Hard working	Misanthropic
Good sense of humor	Bit of a drunk
Goal oriented	

From this list, you come up with what you can do to minimize the aggravations and maximize the aptitudes to better increase your chance at success. In my own case, I dialed back on my drinking, started an exercise program with specific goals in mind (more on that in a later chapter), and structured my free time so that I got a chance to be lazy every once in a while. I also decided that when my misanthropic tendencies were getting the better of me I would turn to humor (either watching comedy or finding the funny side of things) to counteract the potential risk of lashing out at my fellow human beings. All of these combined has led to a much happier and healthier me.

To be fair, a list such as the above is only the first step in the journaling process. The next step is achieved by seeing how your aptitudes and aggravations play out in your day to day life. This is achieved by first tracking what you do now on a daily basis over a specific set of time. Two weeks is usually a good length to start with. Start keeping track of what you do with your time each and every day. All of this information should be recorded in a journal. This journal will take several forms as you progress. To get started you will need to create a baseline journal in order to understand where you are at now.

Exercise 2: The Baseline Journal

When journaling yourself I recommend noting the following:

1) When did you get up?
2) What did you eat/drink during the day (this should include any controlled substances)?
3) What did you plan on doing that day vs. what did you actually accomplish (if anything)?
4) Who did you interact with? How did those interactions make you feel?
5) How much time was "wasted" - i.e. not directed towards a specific goal.
6) How much time was spent working for someone else?[4]
7) Your mood at specific times (at awakening, at lunch, at the end of work, bedtime).[5]
8) What time did you go to bed?

As mentioned above, this exercise will last two weeks. You will need to update your journal several times during your normal waking day. I generally recommend once in the

---

[4] If you are a student, this can be changed to "How much time was spent studying."
[5] This should obviously be modified to fit your own lifestyle as not everyone is a 9-5 person. Roughly the points in time reflect when you get up, at the midpoint of your day, when work is done, and at the end of your day.

morning, once around midday, once in the afternoon/evening, and finally again at bed. If you've got a really good memory, you can just update it before you go to sleep, but most of us are not always paying attention during the day, so it's helpful to jot down notes as we go along.

Once your journal is compiled, it will give you your current personal baseline: a snapshot in time of who you are now based on your actions, interactions, and feelings. From that baseline, you can start to take control and implement change. However, the baseline must come first, and the examination must be brutal. By this I mean that you have to do something that many find impossible — you have to be HONEST with yourself. Ruthlessly so. As cliche as it sounds, your greatest enemy is yourself, but once you know yourself thoroughly, you'll be able to take the steps to overcome yourself and build new selves.

Exercise 3: Introducing Kaizen

In order to commence the process of building a new self (and later, selves), you will need to establish attainable goals. Ask yourself the following: What habits do I want to delete or modify? What do I want to achieve financially? What do I want to achieve romantically? Creatively? What collection of circumstances would maximize my own pleasure and satisfaction and on the other hand, minimize my discomfort and pain? Generally, one determines to see oneself in a new "role" — one where you are engaging in and acting out (in essence) a new life.

The last thing I want to discuss before moving onto the next chapter is the following: one of the ironies of life is that most of us can envision a number of these potential future selves, but we avoid taking the steps to achieve them. I do not believe this is rooted in the idea that we are bad people or unworthy of obtaining our goals, but that we have internalized bad strategies; we try and avoid pain and seek out pleasure, but have sabotaged ourselves by seeking out the easier, short-lived pleasures. While that pushes off immediate pain, it also just stores up larger and larger amounts for later. Additionally, the habits formed due to this phenomenon (or with this behavior) become progressively more and more entrenched in our psyches and thus harder and harder to overcome as time goes on.

Fortunately, there is a way out, of which I personally can take no credit. However, I can at least inform others of a crucial tool in improving their own situations: Kaizen – the Japanese technique of "better way". At its most useful and basic level, it's incremental improvement, but with a twist; it's also about creating new habits that supplant our old ones. In essence, when you want to start something new, do the smallest possible increment of it first, but do that increment every day. As a result, a new habit will take root. As it does, the increment of activity or effort can be increased, again, by the minimum next step. While this takes time, it has the great reward of changing behaviors so imperceptibly that the part of our brains which sabotages massive new undertakings after only a short while is successfully bypassed.

Here's a couple of examples of how Kaizen works: Let's say you determined to start a daily meditation. First, select a time to do so that is fixed. Second, go to the location that you will meditate at that selected time. Third, sit in your meditative posture. That's it, you're done. Next day do the same but after assuming your meditative posture meditate for 1 minute. The next day, meditate for 2 minutes. And so on and so forth. Always meditating at the same time in the same place but each day adding one more minute. Or let's say you've decided to start an exercise program. First, select a time to do so that is fixed. Second, go to the location that you will exercise at that selected time. Third, sit or stand where you exercise. That's it, you're done. The next exercise day do the same but add 1 rep of each exercise you are going to do.[6] The third exercise day do 2 reps of each exercise. And so on and so forth.

Two things are going on here with the Kaizen method: First - the repetition of time and place becomes habit forming. Second - by starting with the smallest possible increment of any activity and then slowly building up one is not overwhelmed at that start. The marathon runner doesn't begin their training by trying to run 26 miles and failing over and over again until they make it to 26 miles. They start with a MUCH shorter distance and then, over time, increase it bit by bit until they can run a marathon.

---

[6] I say next exercise day rather than "next day" because not all exercises programs are by their nature an every day thing. Some are every other day or a set number of days per week (for more see Chapter 4 in this section).

Chapter 2
Trance

There are two primary methods of entering the correct mental state for performing an act of what is typically called "magick". The first is through a process of stilling the mind and senses, colloquially called "trance". This method is best used for the extension of perception. The second, which consists of overloading the mind/senses (known as "ekstasis"), is best used for the extension of will.[7] Authors on the subject of chaos magick, myself included[8], have long made the assertion that these two sides of the same coin: a coin called "gnosis."

Using the word "gnosis" to describe either the complete absence of distracting thoughts/sensations or a state of sensory overload is, in my opinion, bad terminology. Historically, "gnosis" refers to knowing through direct experience/action, specifically a direct **knowing of God**. That is what the original Gnostics meant when they used it. Gnosis to them was a strictly spiritual state of enlightenment. While fascinating, such a state has nothing to do with magick per se.

The only thing that matters in terms of magick is you and the reality you manifest. You discover and create it through the tools of trance and ekstasis. We'll cover ekstasis in the next chapter; let's focus on trance.

Trance occurs on three levels: light, medium, and deep. Deep trance is where the magick happens; though it should be said that a medium trance state can also be used to good effect. A light trance is little more than the

---

[7] Just to be clear—either method can be used, but optimally, trance is used for divination (the supernatural extension of perception), and ekstasis is used for enchantment (the supernatural extension of will).
[8] See my first book: "The Paradigmal Pirate" available through Immanion Press.

beginning of a medium or a deep trance state. The only positive effect of light trance is stress reduction, and it's not useful in terms of manipulating reality.[9] Regarding your practice, the goal should be to obtain a medium to deep trance state on a daily basis. This goal will be reached gradually in stages. These stages refer to the aforementioned Kaizen principle of incremental improvements.[10]

Stage one / Step zero: Start a meditation journal

Begin a journal in which you will track how long you meditate, what sensations, feelings and thoughts arose during meditation, and any "mistakes" or hiccups that occur along the way. Its use becomes clear fairly quickly — you will be able to note progress on a day to day basis. This practice will increase the likelihood of future success. It will allow you at any point to see how far you have come and, indeed, how far you have to go. Your journal can be electronic or physical. Just remember to write in it daily, succinctly covering what transpired during the meditation.

Stage one / Step one: Find the meditative posture that works best for you

In terms of discovering what meditative position works best for you, I recommend the following broad guidelines: First, sit up straight. Regardless of whether you are in a chair, cross legged on the floor, in a Thai posture[11] with a Zafu cushion, or in a half or full Lotus — sit up straight. The

---

[9] Not dissing stress reduction. If you're in a high stress job, daily light meditative trance states can literally save your life.

[10] See the end of Chapter 1 of this Section for an explanation of the Kaizen method.

[11] Hint: Author's fave. See Figure 1 at the end of this chapter.

visualization often encouraged at this point is that of you being pulled up by a thread that rises skywards through your head. Whatever your method, just roll your shoulders back and square them with your head up, eyes level; that's the correct posture. If you have severe back issues, semi-reclined with a support is also totally acceptable, just stay seated. DO NOT attempt to meditate lying down. You will most likely fall asleep, and that's definitely a negative outcome.

Stage one / Step two: Figure out what you're going to do with your hands

There's no right or wrong answer here, apart from not putting your arms into a position where they will fall asleep. Most find resting them gently cupped, open palms facing down on their respective thighs is best. Others like to hold them in a more Buddhist-y fashion over the navel. Just pick what works best for you. Resting on knees, thighs, at waist-level, or over your junk is totally fine. Like with your posture, it's got to be what feels right for you.

Stage one / Step three: Figure out how you're going to track your meditative time

There are two really good options to do this: Either set an alarm clock to go off at your desired finishing time or count to keep track of time silently to yourself. In both situations, it's easy to extend the time you spend meditating either by setting the alarm to a longer duration or by increasing the count. I'll go over the counting method in more detail below. The alarm method sort of speaks for itself. Just keep in mind that if you're going to use the counting method you will still need an alarm for some of the later exercises in this chapter.

Stage two / Step one: Motionlessness

Now that you've figured out what posture and time tracking method will work for you, go ahead and start meditating. Pick a time and place during the day/evening that works for you where you know you won't be disturbed. Hopefully, this will be the same time and location each and every day, but for some that's not an option. In cases where it's not, try and have it occur at a set point after a routine activity, e.g. right after work (whenever work ends), as the first thing done for the day, etc. Regardless, when it's time, turn off your phone / computer / tablet, and be somewhere where you're unlikely to be interrupted.

Start by trying to sit in your meditative posture of choice with your eyes closed for one minute. Again, you can set an alarm and have it go off one minute after you start, or you can close your eyes and count down from 60 (silently, not out loud).[12] Either way, note any extraneous movements, and count them against being motionless. This would include twitching, swallowing, adjusting the position of your hands, legs, arms, etc. Basically, this refers to any voluntary movements that you make. Once you've managed to consistently meditate with no motion, increase your time to two minutes, and then to three, four, and so forth, until you get to 10 minutes.

At this point, you've reached the first goal. Well done. The first goal of a magical meditative/trance practice is 10 minutes of (relative) motionlessness. Obviously, you are breathing; in that sense you are most definitely moving, but apart from breathing, the goal is to reduce the number of non-breathing related movements to zero over a 10

---

[12] I find that this works best with 20 seconds for each breath, 10 in and 10 out but choose what works best for you. For single digits, make them last close to an actual second; count zero-nine, zero-eight, zero-seven, etc.

minute period of time. At this point, most hit a light trance, which is to say a calm relaxed state with slow, regular breathing, and the mind at ease.

If you are using the counting method, you may have noticed that even as you are counting your mind will be capable of a second stream of thought towards the end of the meditative practice. The counting and the second stream of thought are known as cognitive loops, i.e. sections of thought that the mind can manage in parallel. As one progresses, these act as indicators that one is reaching deeper trance states.

Stage two / Step two: Regulation of breathing[13]

Once motionlessness can be maintained consistently for a period of 10 minutes, begin the second stage of slowing down and maintaining a constant rate of breath slower than that of the first 10 minutes. You can do this by having a second alarm which goes off at a period of time after the alarm signifying the end of initial 10 minutes of meditation. Breathing should be from the diaphragm and through the nose, unless you are prevented from doing so because of health, allergy, or other sinus reasons. This is the easiest way. If you were just using an alarm, your breath may have already slowed naturally over the 10 minutes of motionlessness, but at this point, you must take control of the process and will your breath slower.

If you are tracking time via the counting method, you probably counted up to or down from 600 with each breath taking 20 seconds (10 in / 10 out) — if that was the case then slow your breath to 15 in / 15 out with two complete breaths, equating to a minute of extra mediation time.

---

[13] If this is starting to sound familiar, yes, I'm following the pattern Peter Carroll laid out in Liber Null & Psychonaut. Which, by the way, he lifted from Crowley. "If it ain't broke, don't fix it."

Additionally, you may find that 15 in and 15 out becomes easy. If this happens, feel free to do 20 count breaths, remaining mindful that 1 and ½ breaths rather than 2 equals a minute. Some folks can even manage 30 counts at a time, but this takes a bit of practice beyond what's required for our purposes and is entirely optional.

As in the first stage, add a minute at a time beyond the first 10 as you progress in your practice. The goal at this stage is to reach a total of 25-30 minutes: 10 minutes of just motionless plus 15-20 minutes of motionlessness combined with regulation of breathing. As in the earlier stages, you will notice the tendency for your mind to both perform the count or repetitive phrase that you picked and have additional thoughts. As those occur, rather than fighting them, constantly will your attention back to the count. Those other streams of thought (cognitive loops) are a **good** sign. They indicate that you're entering into progressively deeper trance states.

At the end of 25 to 30 minutes, you will have reached a medium trance state. This is good for relaxation, stress reduction, and overall good health, but one further stage is needed. This final stage focuses the mind into a deep trance state — the one conducive to magick.

Stage Three / Step Zero: The Five Deep Trance concentrations

Once in a medium trance state, a deep trance state can be induced by focusing the awareness on an external object, an image in the mind, by repeating a short series of sound at a constant volume and rate (known colloquially as a "mantra"), by beating out a steady, low, constant rhythm on a drum or other surface, or finally, by repeating a short series of choreographed movements with your arms and hands (also known as a "mudra"). As you master each in turn, you will acquire the flexibility to enter into a deep trance state when needed. These techniques can be used in any order; it's all pretty unique to the practitioner. That being said, it shouldn't require hours upon hours to accomplish. If Stage One and Two are done properly, the average individual will obtain a deep trance state in under an hour. That time includes the 25 minutes of Motionlessness and Regulation of Breathing.[14] After establishing and maintaining an effective practice with this method, pick one of the following steps, master it, and move on to another.

Stage Three / Step One: Object Concentration

For Object Concentration, obtain three or four small sheets of blank paper. Post-it notes are ideal, but any regular or lined paper can also be cut down to size. What we are looking for is a 3"x3" / 4"x4" (or for those places "not America", 76mm x 76mm / 101mm x 101mm) piece of paper. On one, draw a simple hollow square; another, a hollow circle; on the third, a hollow equilateral triangle.[15] The size of the shape doesn't really matter, but it should be easy to see from a distance of about two ½ to 3 feet (⅔-1 meter) away, or approximately arms' length.

Assume your meditative posture but orient yourself towards a (preferably) blank wall. The image should be hung or attached to the wall so that it's at eye level for you while seated in your meditative position. In other words,

---

[14] This works out well considering that most people have what is called "a life" that doesn't allow for 3 hours a day meditating. Topping off at 45 minutes to 1 hour is sufficient for the vast majority of people.
[15] These can be filled in and made solid if you want. It all depends on how much time you want to spend scribbling. And yes, you can have rectangles, pentagons, whatever floats your boat, as long as it's a simple shape.

you shouldn't have to strain to see it.[16] Begin your meditation and go through the first 25 minutes normally with your eyes closed. At the 25 minute mark, open up your eyes, and stare neutrally at the shape for 1 minute. If you have slowed your breath using a 15/15 counting method, you can continue at this pace or slow it to 20/20 if you are able. If you are using the alarm method, you will need to set a 3rd alarm to go off 1 minute after the second alarm went off at 25. The objective is to avoid blinking during this meditation.

Once you can do 1 minute of Object Concentration successfully without blinking, take it up to 2 minutes and so forth with an objective of reaching 15-20 minutes.[17] Concentration without blinking is the goal, but a blink here or there is NOT failing. During this time, your eyes will distort this image; resist this. The same goes for your mind. It will attempt to wander off to other thoughts, concerns, and ideas. Resist. Keep the attention focused on the shape. Do this for each of your 3 or 4 shapes in turn. Ideally, you should be able to stare at them without blinking for as long you can manage. This may ultimately be under 10 minutes. That's fine. If you get to 10 or past it, that's great. The primary goal is to be able to stare for a solid block of time beyond a normal person's ability.

This practice is the basis for attaining the ability to scry, reception of occult (i.e. hidden) information about an object, and use of the so called "evil eye". In regards to the first two, the mind in a trance state will naturally recall/remember and correlate information which

---

[16] If you normally wear glasses or contacts, it's ok to wear them during this meditation or any meditation really, but for this one it's important to see clearly at the outset.

[17] If you can't get past 10 minutes of object concentration without blinking do NOT beat yourself up.10 minutes is fine. If you fall short of 10 minutes consistently and find yourself blinking, do NOT beat yourself up. Just shoot for as long as you CAN manage.

otherwise is filtered out during normal interactions and activities or has simply been forgotten over time. As for the third, you're just being creepy.

Stage Three / Step Two: Image Concentration

Image Concentration follows the same basic pattern as Object Concentration, with the notable exception that you are holding the various simple shapes in your mind's eye rather than seeing them and keeping them constantly visualized with your eyes open. That being said, the rest follows a like manner. After you have mastered motionlessness and regulation of breathing, select a series of simple shapes: hollow square, hollow triangle, circle, pentagon, whatever floats your boat. You can go ahead and draw them, or if you did Object Concentration first, recycle the ones you drew. If you did not start with Object Concentration, draw out these shapes so that they fit on something the size of a post-it note as previously mentioned.

Select one of these shapes at random. When you get done with your first 25 minutes of meditation, open your eyes briefly and look at the one you selected. Close your eyes again, and try to visualize it, holding that visualization in your mind's eye for one minute. As before, keep track of time by either a pre-set alarm or by continuing your regulation of breathing count length. After you can hold it for a minute, proceed to two, three, and so forth, with the goal of being able to hold an image in your mind's eye for up to 15-20 minutes.[18]

Mastering Image Concentration is primarily a method

---

[18] Note that I say hold an image in your minds' eye. Not necessarily "hold it steady in your minds eye" - for some holding it steady is, in fact, the easier way. Others retain the image more readily if they allow it to move slightly in a 3d fashion.

used to construct and implant a sigil[19] without the use of any tools save your own body/mind. It's also a way to access specific lost information, much like scrying, but without the physical thing or tool that one would normally have. Finally, it's a great way to focus on an intention for a lucid dreaming session, but more on that later.

Stage Three / Step Three: Sound Concentration

Sound Concentration is the use of a repeating sound uttered by the practitioner to enter into a deep trance state. This sound, or series thereof, is also commonly referred to as a "Mantra" and is used by various schools of meditation for the same end goal: deep trance. However, for the toxic magician, the goal isn't any sort of enlightenment. Rather, it serves a more practical nature. To master this technique, select a long string of words, of roughly four to eight syllables. Preferably, they won't have any deeper meaning. Though if you are using anything from simple words to popular mantras taken from Eastern religions, they will generally have a modicum of meaning. Their meaning is inconsequential when it comes to this practice. I recommend starting off with something like "Alpha, Beta, Charlie, Delta" [20]

As with all the concentrations, begin by mastering the 25 minutes of motionlessness and regulation of breathing. At the 25 minute point, go ahead and start your mantra, and continue chanting it for one minute. Those who have used the breath-count method at this point should switch to having an alarm, starting at the same point. With chanting being fairly easy, it's ok to jump right from 1 minute the first session to 5 the second, 10 the third, and so forth up to 15 or 20 minutes. The goal while chanting is to

---

[19] An encoded intention in visual form.
[20] The first four letters of the NATO phonetic alphabet for A, B, C, D.

keep the mind focused on the chant itself and not let it wander. Additionally, the chant should not change speed or volume.

Of course, if you have reached a deep trance state, your mind will be capable of forming a secondary or even several independent lines of thought. Should this happen, return focus from to the chanting itself. Mantras can also be used as sigils used to empower an encoded intention. However, the sigil-mantra is ultimately used to divine the answer to a question. As deep trance is reached, the imagery, thoughts, and items that come to mind will often provide answers to the line of inquiry one has the intention of divining. Deep trance achieved by all the concentrations used to extend one's perception, circumvents the natural filters used by the human system to prevent overload.

Stage Three / Step Four: Drum Concentration

Drums have been used in music, spiritual, and magical practice for thousands of years. While a rapid drumbeat can raise the tempo and energy of a given activity for the purpose of entertainment or signal the climax of an event during a spiritual practice, it can also be used to induce a deep trance state when kept at a steady measured pace for an extended period of time. Much like Sound Concentration, Drum Concentration uses repetition to allow the mind to enter into a deep trance and access information that was normally denied by the reality filter.[21]

---

[21] Normal human consciousness is only made possible by the mind using a "reality filter" — we are bombarded by information of all kinds during the course of any day: sounds, smells, sights, vibrations, etc. — if our minds didn't filter these out we would be unable to perform any task which involved even the tiniest amount of concentration. While this allows us to function, it also results in a lot of things being missed while focusing on what we are doing.

If you don't own a drum, there are always options at hand. Overturned buckets, boxes, and just about any medium size hollow object can be used. In the absence of objects, one can even beat the floor or cup one's hands and bring them together in a slow clap. After completing the 25 minutes of motionlessness and regulation of breathing, begin beating out a slow, steady rhythm on your medium of choice with either your hands or a drumstick (if you have one lying around). As with the mantra, the goal is to keep a steady, unvarying pace and volume. This control is key to reaching a deep trance state. Similar to Sound Concentration, it's easy to go from one to five to ten to fifteen to twenty in a series of sessions, tracking time while drumming with either the alarm or breath-count method.

Note that drumming can also be combined with the previously listed concentrations and done simultaneously. If you choose to do this, that is entirely up to you. Keep in mind that if you chose to combine methods such as Sound and Drum, both the sound/mantra chosen and the drumming should be performed in a controlled state as mentioned above.[22] Some find that they can continue drumming and chanting for hours and once you have reached the 20 minute mark (45 minutes total meditation), feel free to keep going on at least one occasion. Interesting observations have been known to occur, such as the distortion of one's sense of time or physical space.

Stage Three / Step Five: Mudra Concentration

Mudras are a type of symbolic gesture often used in Eastern religions. In terms of use for attaining trance, Mudra Concentration can be used alone or with the Object, Image, or Sound Concentrations. The goal in creating a

---

[22] It can probably go without saying that if you are combining Sound and Drum Concentration, you're going to use an alarm to determine the length of the Trance session.

mudra is to concentrate and hold the posture of the mudra while keeping its idea or intention (the meaning of the mudra) in mind.

As with all previously mentioned concentrations, begin by mastering the 25 minutes of motionlessness and regulation of breathing. At the 25 minute mark, shift your posture to the mudra you have chosen to work with. I have included 5 basic mudras to start with <see table 1>. The goal is to maintain the gesture for one minute, and then two, and so forth up to 15 - 20 minutes. Either the alarm or the regulation of breathing methods of keeping track of time can be used, unless you decide to engage in a mantra while executing a mudra — then your best bet is to use an alarm.

Table 1

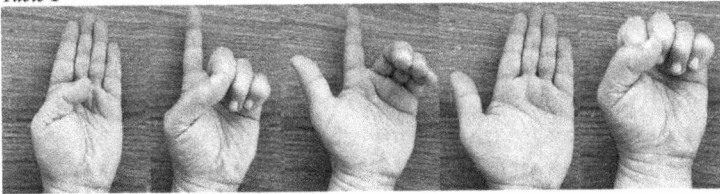

Feel free to come up with your own mudras or use ones that derive from common culture. For example, you can use the peace symbol (as is or reversed to form the English two fingered salute) or hold up both hands in "I have no fucks left to give posture." <see table 2>

Table 2

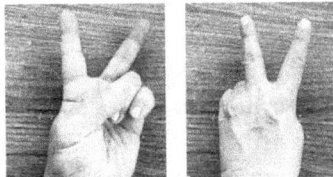

Finally, you can combine mudras to create a repeating series. I recommend the creative W, E, L flowing mudra in which you cycle through the three symbols.[23] This can be done with any other set of mudras. If you are using ones that have a particular meaning, you can combine said meanings in a way to state a more complex intention. Regardless, the goal is ultimately a deep trance state.

The Extension of Perception

The ultimate use of deep trance is the extension of perception. Once you have achieved a deep trance state, you have a number of options or, more precisely, tool sets to work with. Frankly, many practitioners of the occult use these tools incorrectly. It is utterly and totally **useless**, in my estimation, to engage any stranger or associate for the purpose of what is classically called "divination". All this generates is noise, wasting time by throwing out a bunch of guesses about you and your future based on nothing more than what they can glean of you in the limited time they have to perform their divination. Any "success" on their part is more likely the result of just luck.

The exception to the rule of not consulting a stranger or an associate for the intention of extending your perception is to consult one who is also an expert at obtaining a deep trance state. They must be very close in terms of their relationship with you, as it will have been necessary for them to observe the actions, words, and events around you. This would allow them, from a deep trance state, to filter out irrelevant information that would lend to a higher rate of accuracy. However, not even our closest friends and relatives are with us ALL the time, so this too is at risk of falling flat. In short, you're better off doing it on your own.

The tool set you use to extend your perception is irrelevant. You can frame your questioning before going into a deep trance state right before bed and interpret the

---

[23] WhatEverLoser. See Figure 2 at the end of this chapter.

answer from that night's dreams. You can scry them in a crystal ball or a pool of black liquid. You can draw a single random tarot card from a tarot deck. You can throw the I-Ching or rune stones or bones. You can stare at tea leaf residue. You can stare at the lines of your hand, etc. Basically, any method will do.[24] The tool doesn't matter, the deep trance state does.

Is there a proper way to frame your questioning? Yes, it needs to be translated into what is known as a sigil. In short, the question (or intention) is encoded to remove it one level from your conscious awareness. This allows you to focus on obtaining the deep trance state itself rather than on what you are seeking to know.

Your sigil can be rendered in one of the following ways: An image that is generated from the non-duplicate letters of your question; a picture which takes a visual line drawing of your intention and stylizes it; it can be formed into a flowing mudra in which each gesture forms part of its meaning; it can be drummed out in morse code; it can be made into a mantra by rearranging the non-repeating letters into a short phrase or by arranging the letters backwards.[25] These sigils can also be further utilized in the following chapter on Ekstasis.

Once you have your sigil (regardless of the form it takes), perform one of the previously mentioned exercises that you have mastered to obtain a deep trance state. When you have reached the climax and stopped your mantra/mudra/staring/imagining/drumming, engage your selected perception tool and allow your mind to present the images, thoughts, and words that answer your question. Disregard any and all preconceptions, selfish judgements, hopes and/or fears. Record and interpret the results.

---

[24] There are too many classic methods of divination to cover here. Just pick one.
[25] See Figure 3 at the end of this chapter (Mudra example left out for brevity).

Joshua Wetzel

Figure 1: Thai Meditative Posture

Figure 2: W. E. L. Mudra shapes

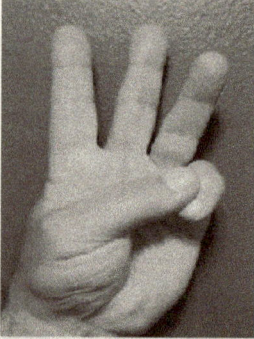

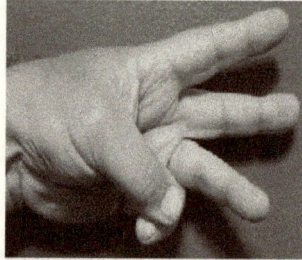

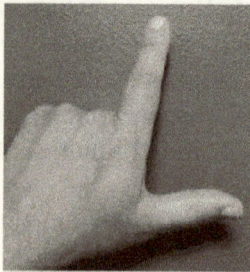

Figure 3:

Image generated from non-duplicate letters:

HOW IS MY DAY GOING TO BE?
HOW IS MY DA GN T B

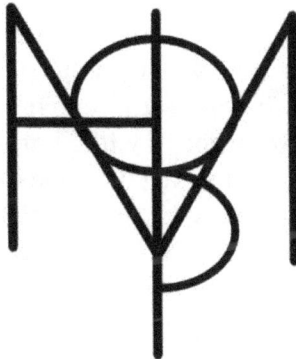

Short phrase example: Tob Gand Mish Wy

Backward mantra example: Eb Ot Gniog Yad Ym Si Woh

Stylized visual line drawing of your intention:

Drummed out in Morse code example:

Chapter 3
Ekstasis

As mentioned in chapter 2, there are two mental states conducive to performing an act of magick. The first is Trance: the stilling of the body/mind to a point of complete quietience. The other mental state is called Ekstasis, which is achieved by whipping oneself into a frenzy. Both can be used for either the extension of perception or the extension of will. That being said, Trance is the optimal state for what is classically known as "divination" or the ability to "prophesy." Ekstasis, on the other hand, is best suited for what is classically known as "enchantment" or the ability to cast a "spell".

Examples of the body/mind states that can lead to Ekstasis are as following: extreme anger/rage, extreme pain, karezza orgasm, extreme fear/terror, prolonged ecstatic dance, glossolalia,[26] mental exhaustion, and hyperventilation. This list is fairly thorough but shouldn't be considered exhaustive. However, it does cover the three main avenues of overloading the system to obtain Ekstasis: emotional overload, mental overload, and physical overload.

Unlike the Trance exercises, there is really no set amount of time that it takes to achieve Ekstasis, as this varies between individuals. The best form of practice is to attempt to increase the time one is in the particular form that would lead to Ekstasis until one achieves it. Keeping in mind that this might both very quick or it might take quite some time and also, depending on multiple factors, it just might not happen. I strongly recommend caution! Know your body and know your limits and do not take any form of Ekstasis to a point of self harm!

People in certain fundamental religious sects who use glossolalia in their worship have noted that it can be

---

[26] Known colloquially as "speaking in tongues".

random and that, until you've achieved Ekstasis, you really won't **know** what that state is, i.e. it can only be known through direct experience and not related in any other way. That being said, a perfect state of Ekstasis is not necessary for an effective magical working. It's only necessary to reach the edge of attenuated consciousness to have an impact. If one can get there, great. If one can't, attempt to push as hard as possible to get there: a methodology commonly known as "fake it until you make it."

I'll go over each of the states in turn and suggest some methods for reaching them. I will also discuss effective methods of framing them within a ritual or, as I prefer to call it, a reality engineering event. Before beginning any such exercise, it's necessary to have formulated a desired event to be accomplished and a method of encoding it (sigil) along with a technique for obfuscating it from your conscious mind. This method of encoding and obfuscation must also include a way to recall, and thus verify, your results (or lack thereof). I will also suggest a working framework for this. Finally, I will mention the ritual use of entheogenic chemicals vis-a-vis altered states of consciousness, as to leave them out would be both remiss of me and a tad hypocritical. We'll begin with the physical.

Routes to Physical Ekstasis:

Method One - Pain

Human evolution has resulted in, as far as I can tell, a unique relationship between individuals in our species and pain that is not experienced by them. Which is to say, the human body/mind system has developed coping methods to deal with pain which have given rise to the whole phenomenon of BDSM culture. While other species simply avoid pain, some human beings will seek it out in order to experience the endorphin laden post pain period of recovery. In this, they've turned the coping method that the body/mind uses to deal with the adverse experience of pain and its aftermath into an end goal in and of itself.[27]

The four main types of pain used to achieve Ekstasis in the context of a ritual are: flagellation, blunt force, cutting, piercing, or some combination thereof. Pain as a route to an altered state of consciousness is evidenced throughout the ancient and modern world in cults, sects, and religions. Just about every belief system has some subset of devotees who will engage in a, usually, self directed form of self-harm as a means to express devotion or obtain enlightenment. It is also used to become closer to the spirit world or entity that they worship.

Three of the four methods mentioned (flagellation, cutting, and piercing) require a tool of some sort: whips, flails, and floggers are typically used for flagellation; knives and razors can be used for cutting; needles, thorns, and pins are required for piercing. With the remaining utilization of blunt force pain, a paddle or other blunt instrument (baseball bat, cricket bat, baton, etc.) can be used, but you can also just be hit with a clenched fist or open hand.

The best method for any of the above methods is self directed, as opposed to being struck, cut, or poked, by someone else. During this time, you should remain focused on the intention of the reality engineering event. The pain inflicted drives other thoughts and ideas from the mind, thus allowing one to focus on a sigil or chant or some other form of enchantment.

Method Two - Karezza

Bringing oneself (or one's partner) to the edge of orgasmic

---

[27] I'm not suggesting that everyone into a BDSM lifestyle is an endorphin junkie. There are many other elements to it, but that one is definitively there.

release, but not crossing over to it, is referred to as Karezza. However, in a magical context, this technique is used to dance on the edge of orgasm before finally crossing over in order to charge the intention. Orgasm in and of itself can sometimes be sufficient if the experience is intense enough. Regardless, used in conjunction with Karezza, an orgasm is a useful way to charge a sigil. Some prefer to use this method only in the context of intentions which involve creation (Such as creating a Tulpa or Eidolon[28]), but there is no real limit or restriction on what type of intent you use for this particular method.

Method Three - Dance

Driving oneself to the edge of physical exhaustion, without running a marathon, can be obtained through ecstatic dance. Handily, the movements within the dance can be mudra based, or the practitioner can chant a mantra or focus on a drawn sigil placed in a prominent location while the dance takes place. Drumming can also be used (especially effective in groups) to set the pace. With multiple participants the drummers themselves may be focused on Trance while the dancer or dancers are focused on Ekstasis. While lending itself to a group exercise, solitary dancing is also (if not more) effective.

Method Four - Hyperventilation

Rapid shallow breathing (hyperventilation) increases the amount of oxygen in your circulatory system while reducing the amount of carbon dioxide. In doing so, it upsets the normal balance. This method is often automatically triggered if the Emotional method of fear is engaged. Regardless, the goal in using hyperventilation is

---

[28] Referred to classically as a servitor or familiar.

to come close to blacking out but not actually doing so. Use this physical method with caution. It can be used, as mentioned, in conjunction with fear and can also be used with the other excitatory methods (dance, karezza and pain). Usually the only type of sigil used while practicing this method is a pictogram or drawn sigil.

Routes to Emotional Ekstasis:

Method One - Anger (Rage)

It should surprise no one, in my opinion, that an extreme state of anger is a route to Ekstasis. Almost every individual has, at one time or another, experienced the sensation of being so angry that they were "seeing red." This level of anger is what is required to charge one's intention in an Ecstatic ritual. Generally, it's obtained by focusing intently on a hated subject, whether that be a person, some form of injustice, or humiliation — doesn't really matter. What matters is willfully building the state up to a frenzy of hatred until all other thoughts and considerations are driven from the mind. A good assist for obtaining this state is aggressive, loud, fast, repetitive music.

Visually represented sigils are best utilized for this method. Rage is built up until it totally consumes the practitioner and then, at the climax, the sigil is destroyed. The other types (mudra or mantra) can be used similarly in the mind's eye — practical, but not ideal; It is best to have a physical representation to destroy.[29]

Method Two - Fear (Terror)

Total terror can focus the mind completely or, if taken too far, paralyze it. Paralyzing fear combined with focus on the

---

[29] And that is far more satisfying anyway.

intention can be used in a ritual context. It is possible (and some would say, preferable) to work this type by yourself. Usually, you have to place yourself into an appropriate context, late at night, isolated with additional mechanisms at the ready to induce the state. Trusted individuals can be used to assist in a group context, but there are enough props out there to allow the individual to induce the state on their own.

Not everyone has the same triggers that result in being afraid; each person is a unique subject when it comes to what truly scares them. The best resource in this case is you yourself for creating a safe situation in which you can still terrorize yourself. Any type of sigil can be used.

Routes to Mental Ekstasis:

Method One - Glossolalia

Also known as "speaking in tongues" — glossolalia involves the use of rapid-fire verbal babble to induce a state of Ekstasis. Generally, one starts out with random vowel and consonant sounds or even random words. As one progresses, the stream of noise gets faster and faster until an Ecstatic state is reached. This can take quite some time and, similar to the Trance states, the objective is to maintain a steady flow once the individual is "at speed" (so to speak) in generating the meaningless string of word-like noises. Any attempt by the mind to wander should be suppressed and the attention focused back on the generation of babble.

Glossolalia can also fall into a word-salad pattern; this has been known to be used by practitioners functioning in a group to generate a shared word or phrase. Obviously a mantra type sigil is the best used during this process, though one can also engage in glossolalia while drumming or dancing.

Method Two - Sensory Overload

A state of Ekstasis can be generated by overwhelming the mind with cognitive input: a rapid intake of visual, auditory, and other stimuli. The Ekstatic state is, in this instance, generated by the mind trying to make sense of what is going on and repeatedly failing or of solving equations or puzzles with too short of a time allotted to complete them. To overload the senses takes a great amount of work and is usually assisted by doing so in conjucture with a chemical (read drug) aid, which will be touched on at the end of this chapter.

Constructing a framework for a reality engineering event

Now that you have an idea of the many ways to reach Ekstasis, the obvious question is: "How best do I use this to obtain results?" The answer is to put it to use within a reality engineering event commonly referred to as a ritual. What you will need to execute this is:

1) a space in which you won't be disturbed
2) your intention encoded in such a way as to be obscured to the conscious mind (i.e. a sigil)
3) a method of Ekstasis (preselected)
4) a way to verify your results (or lack thereof)
5) things left out

That's pretty much it. Actual magic doesn't require anything else. You don't need candles, robes, incense, wands, or any of the other knick-knacks occultists are so fond of. Nor do you need long winded invocations, banishings or statements of intent. You just really, at the base of it, need you; everything else is window dressing.

That being said, let us go over the 4 things you do need and put them together for the required framework.

Space.

First find an area where you won't be disturbed. This can be anywhere; it doesn't have to be a location dedicated to magic. It can be a spare room, an exercise room, even a bedroom or living room. Nor does it need to be located indoors. If privacy can't be obtained where you live, you can always go outdoors. Parks and wilderness areas often have locales that are seldom, if ever, visited. Abandoned structures or rented space works as well. Regardless, just find somewhere where you can be alone or relatively alone.[30]

Encoded Intention.

In the journaling chapter you created a number of objectives. These can be turned into sigils using one of the methods described in chapter 2. Once you have these you can execute them using Ekstasis during a reality engineering event. I recommend generating a number of them and then selecting one at random to "fire off" as it were. Use only one per ritual.

Ekstasis.

With your space available and sigil on hand, begin by performing a basic meditation of 25 minutes (10 minutes motionlessness, 15 of regulation of breathing), after which

---

[30] Sometimes there is privacy, but it's only semi-privacy, and there are noise concerns. In cases such as these, one solution is to tell roommates or neighbors that you've joined an avante garde theatre group (or a band) and you're rehearsing a scene (or song) that involves a type of ritual in the play.

point start the excitatory practice of your choice to whip yourself up into a state of Ekstasis. Once you feel you have gotten to that point, destroy the sigil. If it's a picture, burn it or rip it up. If you've been chanting a mantra, making a mudra, or even tapping out a morse code drum beat while performing an ecstatic activity, force yourself to laugh.[31] It works well to help you return to the mundane. Some folks also have been known to flip on the radio or television, thus changing the frame of reference so rapidly that the sigil is forgotten.

Verification.

There is no use in going through all this if you have no idea if you are succeeding or not. Yet, it's key to keep the desired objective out of the conscious mind for maximum effectiveness. How then does one verify results? Simple enough: another method of encoding. As you write up your sigils, copy their intentions out in the back of your journal, or in a separate location, using a simple replacement method of encoding (such as replacing letters for numbers, A=1, B=2 etc.). Alongside this entry, inscribe an unencoded date at which you'll decode what you've recorded and determine if you were successful or not. I personally set a time frame of six months in the future for verification, but you can set it for a time that seems reasonable to you: a year, a month, three months, etc.

Left out.

Some people familiar with doing more classical rituals will note that I've left out things that might be considered "key" elements; a lot of rituals involve a "banishing"

---

[31] You can also force yourself to laugh at the end of burning a pictorial sigil too. It's a good way to change gears rapidly.

before and after the ritual and a "statement of intent". These actions are counterproductive and unnecessary in my experience. Those who perform "banishings" state that you're moving from "real life" to "pretend" (i.e. magick) and back again. The "statement of intent" is often worded in such a way that it brings your objective firmly into your conscious mind, and that is counterproductive.

I believe that engineering your reality should be **part** of your reality, not divorced from it. Skip activities like banishing and lighting candles and incense or ringing bells, etc. That just sets the activity apart and dis-integrates it from your life. Keep your magic integrated with your reality. The "statement of intent" brings the objective to the fore of your consciousness; thus one is tempted to then fantasize about the result or outcome. This, in my experience, takes the reality creating energy away from your objective and squanders it in fantasy. So refrain from pronouncing your intentions before you start.

Chemicals
(A note on stimulants, depressants, & hallucinogens)

The use of mind-altering substances and the practice of magic, spirituality, and religion is well known and documented, so I won't go over it here. For our purposes, the two main types of drugs which come into potential play for our purposes are stimulants and depressants. The former can be used to assist in obtaining a state of Ekstasis, while the latter can be used in conjunction with Trance. Others (such as hallucinogens) tend to either overwhelm and become a thing in and of itself, or do not prove to be of any use when executing a reality engineering event.

Depending on your location, many (if not all) chemical options may be illegal for you to obtain and use (not that this has ever stopped anyone). Just be aware that if you are going to use them, you're doing so at your own risk. They are not necessary or required in any way, shape, or form for doing magick. Since some of them carry the risk of addiction for people who are predisposed to it, avoidance may be the best route to go.

Chapter 4
Exercise (Physical Control)

The ultimate goal of setting off on an exercise program should not be to lose weight. Nor should it be to acquire the strength, used to strive against others in any competitive sports, getting in shape, or obtaining the increased energy and confidence that often comes with success. No, the ultimate goal of exercise is control of one's own body and its capabilities. Through exercise, the body becomes another weapon in the toxic magician's arsenal to be used to assert control of oneself and one's environment when required.

While not the primary focus, the downsides to being out of shape are numerous. Physicians understandably harp on about health issues, but from a practical standpoint, the main downside is not having the energy or strength to get anything meaningful done. If you have set out goals to accomplish after performing chapter 1 and journaling yourself, being in shape will benefit you by giving you the energy to reach those goals. The mind can conceive of many things you desire; the body/mind is the engine that gets you to the point of possessing (and keeping) those things. I say body/mind because they are intertwined in a chemical/hormonal way that ties ideas to actions and vice versa. In the symbiotic entity that is every human, if the body portion isn't optimal, then the mind would be akin to an experienced captain piloting a leaky rowboat. More energy is wasted keeping afloat than actually going anywhere.

I will lay out what has worked for me in order to provide an example of an exercise program. Don't feel like this is the only option; obviously, you must find what works for you in your present circumstances and go with that. Regardless of which form of physical self improvement you choose, utilize the Kaizen approach to assist in turning your initial efforts into ingrained habit. Gradually, constantly, and steadily improve from there. I also recommend tying this practice with the Trance work in Chapter 2. For myself, meditation shortly or immediately after working out has made getting into and out of a meditative posture easier.[32] Older people, such as myself, sometimes have the joy of a leg or legs falling asleep during meditation. Increased blood flow from working out lessens the probability of that happening.

What has worked for me is the 5x5 workout pioneered by Reg Park combined with the aforementioned Kaizen approach of incremental improvement. They function together quite well, especially if you have never undertaken a workout program before. You can start at any level and consistently move forward from that point. I'll explain how they work together below. Starting from ground zero is the best way to illustrate this methodology, rather than where I actually started from. If you already work out, or have a program, you don't have to begin from nothing. Instead, you can start from any point that you're accustomed to using what is outlined below.

Day Zero: pick which 5x5 you want to go with and select a starting weight

There are a number of 5x5 workouts to choose from. The one I chose to go with was this one:

StrongLifts 5x5 Week 1		
Monday - workout A	Wednesday - workout B	Friday - workout A
Squat 5x5	Squat 5x5	Squat 5x5
Bench Press 5x5	Overhead Press 5x5	Bench Press 5x5
Barbell Row 5x5	Deadlift 1x5	Barbell Row 5x5

[32]. Though if you're drowning in sweat, freaking feel free to take a shower between working out and meditating.

StrongLifts 5x5 Week 2		
Monday	Wednesday	Friday
Squat 5x5	Squat 5x5	Squat 5x5
Overhead Press 5x5	Bench Press 5x5	Overhead Press 5x5
Deadlift 1x5	Barbell Row 5x5	Deadlift 1x5

33

I also went online and watched how to properly perform each of the 5 StrongLifts in terms of maintaining a proper form. If you have access to a personal trainer, or someone with lifting experience, they can show you the best form. Otherwise, there are online videos or books available that show how to maintain proper posture.

I selected 50lbs (22kg for not-America) to start with, as I could comfortably lift that amount without any strain. Keep in mind, you can start with 0lbs — just the bar.[34] There is thus no minimum, really. I also noted that most workout programs talk about "going to the gym" — personally, I got a bench and weights and did it all at home. Being the cheap bastard that I am, I got them secondhand. However, if a gym is more cost effective, and some are quite reasonable in terms of price, go that route.

My apologies if all of this is coming from an entitled perspective and you find yourself in a position where you lack access to either a) a weight set, or b) a gym membership. It is possible to also design a workout without equipment and a quick search online will result in many resources to help you construct a workout using just your body.

---

[33] Medhi: Stronglifts 5x5 Workout - (online, https://stronglifts.com/5x5/).
[34] A barbell itself can weigh up to 45lbs (20kg), some are less, I believe the one I have only weighs about 5 or 10 lbs (2 or 4.5kg).

Day 1: Just sit

Exactly what it says. Put on your workout clothes, go to the location that you will workout, and just sit a moment. That's it. The idea here is to begin the habit by going to the location that you will exercise. The process of going there, in and of itself, is a start. It doesn't matter if it's a gym or a room in your residence. You've begun the process by just going to where it will happen.

Day 2[35]: One of each

Go to the location that you are going to workout and perform one of each set. For the 5x5 listed above, that would be one squat, one overhead press, and one deadlift (i.e. Wednesday's workout). That's it. Go about your day. The only other consideration is that the time you go each day should either be the same or within the same time frame − if you decide to workout after work and your work time varies, always try and workout in the same time frame. For example, if you workout an hour after getting off work, it doesn't matter if that is 6 PM, 7 PM, or later; what matters is the time between getting off work and the time you workout should stay the same.

Day 3: Two of each

Go to the location that you are going to workout and perform two of each set. For the 5x5 listed above, it would be two squats, two bench presses and two barbell rolls (i.e. Friday's workout). Again, the time you go to workout should match the time or the time frame of days one and two.

---

[35] Note for the 5x5, it's every other day; if you started on a Monday, that would make day 2 a Wednesday.

Day 4 and onwards

This progresses into week two, in which you would progress with three sets of each (day 4), four sets of each (day 5), and five sets of each (day 6). At any point during this progression, you can go to the full number if you feel you are ready, i.e. 5 sets of 5 each which is a total of 25 of each of the exercise types for that day. If you feel capable, a full set can be done at any point between doing 1x5 (day 6) and what would be scheduled to be 4x5, but I do have some recommendations.

First of all, if you manage to get up to 15 of each type in a day (3x5), you're probably ready to go to the full 5x5. Secondly, listen to the feedback your body is giving you; if you feel slightly sore on the off days in between sessions, that's good. However, if you're sore and stiff on the day after the day off (the next day of working out), then you may have overdone it, and you need to take it down a bit.

Once you are doing 5x5 at your minimum weight without any difficulty, it's time to increase the weight. Usually, this is done in 5lb increments while keeping the number of repetitions and sets the same. As you master each 5lb increase, continue adding another 5 until you plateau or you reach your goal (I set a goal of going from 50 to 150lbs in a year and accomplished that). If you plateau and can't seem to add another 5lbs to your working weight, there are a number of variations to continue your progression.

One technique you can use is to drop the amount you lift in half, but double the repetitions, and then take that up a notch in rotation. So, instead of doing 5x5 you do 5x10 but at half the normal weight. Do that for a time period of two weeks before going back to the 5x5 at your maximum weight. Then, slowly increase the amount of the half-weight weeks. So, a routine where your maximum is 100lbs might look like this:

Two weeks 5x5 at 100lbs.

Two weeks 5x10 at 50lbs.

Two weeks 5x5 at 100lbs.

Two weeks 5x10 at 55lbs.

Two weeks 5x5 at 100lbs.

Two weeks 5x10 at 60lbs.

Etc.

Another recommendation I have if you have plateaued at a certain weight or don't feel you need to increase your weight is to slow the rate that you perform the exercise by half. A final technique would be to shorten the rest you take between sets. If you are taking two minutes between one set and the next, drop that to one minute; if you are taking one minutes between one set and the next, drop that wait down to 30 seconds, etc. Mix and match the above to keep things challenging.

What about a weightlifting belt? Should you get one? The short answer is "no" — the long answer is "yes, when it's required". For most people, the recommendation I've seen is the following, but please feel free to consult a physical trainer if you have one available: You only need a weightlifting belt when you can squat your body weight, deadlift one and a half times your body weight, and shoulder press three-quarters of your body weight. Before you can do that, you don't need a weightlifting belt. However, you may wish to fudge 5 or 10lbs lighter than the general recommendation from my experience.

What about cardio (Running, biking, etc.)? Is that a good way to go? Yes. If weightlifting isn't your thing, you can engage in cardio exercise instead. The same general principles apply in terms of getting started. First, just go to where you are going to do it. Second, do a very short amount or distance, with the object of increasing the distance or intensity incrementally until you get up to your goal amount. This isn't my area of expertise (though I used to do a lot of biking), and I found that the same principles of Kaizen applied to doing it right, e.g. I biked a mile one day, then two the next day, then five a few days later, and then 10, before finally being able to bike the 12.5 miles to work and back, weather permitting. That can be a downside to any exercise done outdoors: the weather can screw with you. So, if you can stay inside, stay inside.

Sticking with the exercises listed above, gradually improving via the Kaizen method of incremental progress, will lead to being in control of your physical body and will habitualize the notion that the body is a tool that you shape. This is especially true in regard to when you have reached your main goal weight and begin playing with the types of lifting that you do. As you do this, be mindful of the control you are exerting over yourself. Only you have that control. Keep that in mind.

Epilogue 1: Working out Without Equipment

It's not always possible to purchase or gain access to specialized equipment for working out. However, it is always possible to work out if you can set aside at least 30 minutes, 3 to 4 times a week. Your own body and a little physics can be used to increase strength and stamina with these exercises below. Obviously I did not come up with any of them as they are all very common. However, I felt it good to put them there as a resource rather than make folks go out and hunt for them.

As with the 5x5 program one should start off slowly, one step at a time. Increasing incrementally until a full workout program is achieved.

Push-ups (1 minute / diamond / fingertip / super / military)
Sit-ups & crunches
Burpees
Plank & Plank reach under.

(For non-1st world situations where you can't get weights or go to the gym).

https://www.healthline.com/health/fitness-nutrition/no-weight-workout#12

Chapter 5
Emotional Control

The previous three chapters have, for the most part, dealt with control on a physical level. Apart from certain elements of Ekstasis, exercise and Trance establish firm control over your body and its rhythms, turning the body from a passive tool to an active one at your disposal. Emotional control consists of taking the first steps out of that entirely internal zone and into one where social elements come into play. Mastering your emotions is central to future success.

One of the main characteristics setting the toxic magician apart from all others, practitioners and non-practitioners alike, is their ironclad control over their emotional states. Our emotions (we all have them, apart from a few psychopaths), are potentially our greatest weakness. There are entire categories of people who make their living off manipulating the emotional states of others in order to get what they want, rather than what is in their own best interest. If your emotions are firmly under your control, they lose all power to control you, and the tables are flipped.

Keep in mind that emotional control doesn't mean bottling your emotions up or suppressing them entirely. To do that would only lead to them coming out at inappropriate times and places. You have to have a safety valve, a release. However, even that regulated expression of emotion should be kept under your control. Whether with a psychologist that you visit on a regular basis, a friend or partner with whom you are free to "vent", or just a soundproof room that you can go into and scream into the void, it should be at the time and place of your choosing. The outlet, like your emotions themselves, should be under your control.

The "quick and dirty" regarding emotions is this: when you are in public, never fly off the handle in anger or break down sobbing in sorrow. Even excessive displays of happiness and affection should be avoided. Basically, anything which would fall under the category of "emotional outburst" should be assiduously avoided. Only that which is considered "socially acceptable" in terms of emotional reaction should be expressed in front of others. Additionally, never get caught out in public blind drunk or severely bent out of shape by a drug.

The reason for this should be obvious: a person, out in the open, in any of these conditions is no longer in control. Don't put yourself or allow yourself to be put into one of these states. To do so is like painting a giant target on your front and back, akin to saying, "This person is vulnerable and is the perfect mark to be manipulated." The less scrupulous around you will take advantage, and don't think for a moment that this group of predators excludes those you now consider your "friends".

Conversely speaking, individuals who have lost control of themselves in public can be manipulated by you if there is something that you desire from them or wish to learn from them. When resistance is down, anything and everything just might be in play.[36] Though, be aware, there may be consequences if you take the opportunity of exploitation too far. This is especially true with people with whom you might have to have future interactions.

Finally, emotional outbursts should be avoided, not just in person, but also online. The internet is a wasteland of wrecked reputations. It is festooned with people who couldn't control their reactions and who wrote or said things that they couldn't take back. This includes some who thought their anonymity was assured. It often is not.

---

[36] Though what comes out might lack, well, coherence. It can still be parsed into useful information.

Don't play in that sewer; you'll only wind up smelling like shit.

Gaining control of your emotions can be accomplished by learning, practicing, and executing the following exercises. Once they become a habit ingrained into your psyche, you'll not only be able to keep your emotions under control but also spot when others are trying, intentionally, to disrupt your peace of mind (and the peace of mind of those around you). Finally, you will gain the ability to turn the tables, if necessary, on those attempting to throw you off balance and take advantage of you.

Exercise 1: Become the passive journaler & listener

This exercise is a partial extension of Chapter 1. Here you will be turning the rigorous attention that you first used on yourself onto those around you, not to gain control over them, but to catalogue how those who move in your social, family, and working circles express themselves. First, you will look for personality types and some broad characterizations: Which of them, if any, are you genuinely happy to be around? Which of them is depressed or tends to depress you when you interact? Who pisses you off? Why do they piss you off? Which associate (or associates) is a drunk? An addict?[37] Do you know any workaholics? Who is the gossip of the group? Who is the drama-llama?[38] Who is the "trusted friend" that everyone relies on? Who is in love with, or attracted to, whom?

Do this for a month with all of those people that you come into regular (not fleeting) contact with. Apart from simply observing diligently, take the time to listen to what each and every one of them has to say. Keep the focus off

---

[37] "Never trust a junkie" (Ministry, Psalm 69, "just one fix".)

[38] For some of these, odds are if you can't figure which of them it is...it just might be YOU.

of you and on them. Refrain from talking about yourself except in the smallest of ways. It's not necessary to have a "heart-to-heart" talk with everyone you know, just enough to allow them to monopolize as much of the conversation as they like.

You will gain valuable information. Take note of it mentally, and then keep a record of it, but only in a location that can NOT be accessed by anyone but yourself. This should NOT be a permanent record, just one retained long enough for you to memorize and then destroy. I can't emphasize this enough — do NOT let anyone know you are studying them. Do NOT let anyone see a detailed analysis of them, no matter how tempting. It won't make them feel important that you are analyzing them; it will just creep them out, and they will close themselves off to you. This is the opposite of what you need to happen for this practice to have any long-term value.

Take your time. That's part of the reason I recommend at least a solid month for the duration of this exercise. Do not try to wring every detail out of every person every time you interact with them. Take information in at a reasonable rate. This will prevent what you are doing from appearing suspicious to your friends and acquaintances. Most of the time, when it's more than just you and one other person, you can allow the others to do most of the talking. That way, you're not asking a thousand questions. Once you've completed your observation and memorized and roughly categorized everyone, move on to the next exercise.

Exercise 2: Detachment and Delay

Arguments are often started, not because of what someone has said, but from an overly quick reaction to what has been said. This leads to a subsequent response with things spiraling out of control. For this exercise, you will gradually eliminate this possibility by both delaying any response and adopting a detached perspective on what was said or written that might set you off. Keeping your emotions under your firm control is very much about driving them rather than them driving you.

This can be practiced first in non-argumentative situations and exchanges. Starting with your next casual conversation, pause whenever asked for your opinion or any feedback. Simply count to 5 in your head. Then, respond in a measured way. During that first pause, consider your answer carefully, even if that answer is to a simple question. Try to do this just once on the first day and in just one conversation. On the second day, do it twice and so forth, until by the end of the month you are doing it for every response.

If you do come across someone who is actively hostile and interrogatory, immediately put the delay into practice combined with detachment. Detachment, in this case, is simply not viewing the question or statement as intended for you. In other words, it is as if you were witnessing the exchange you are having with the person but from outside of yourself. When doing so, and during a pause of 5 to 10 seconds before responding, think about what the best response would be if you were someone else having that exchange with the hostile or upset individual.

A good way to get started on detachment is to actually remember the last negative exchange or argument you had with someone. Go over what you said (or screamed/shouted) to the other person and picture what would have been a better response. Imagine one that would de-escalate rather than further inflame the confrontation.

Another approach to detachment is to put yourself in the shoes of the hostile party. Consider why they might be upset with you. Try to see things from their perspective before you respond. Again, the delay factor is important here. If you've practiced the delayed response as suggested above, it should have become routine, allowing you time to assess where the other person is coming from before reflexively attacking them. This will not only help you keep in control of your emotions but of the conversation itself. A shouting match or a barrage of insults might momentarily feel good but, in the long run, It's counterproductive. Even total strangers might, at some point, be a resource you can tap. That advantage is squandered if you fly off the proverbial handle at anyone with whom you have a disagreement.

Exercise 3: Identification, Reduction and Reframing and what is driving the other

The next exercise in controlling your emotions is all about identifying why something might trigger you into a hostile response and reducing the probability of that by reframing what was said or written. Like exercise 2, revisit the last series of fights you have had online or in person, and try to narrow down the point at which you lost control or that the discussion spiraled into a pointless argument.

Did the other party you were talking to or interacting with use a "trigger word" such as an ethnic, sexual or racial slur? Make an outlandish statement? Did they use either false equivalency or an exaggerated slippery-slope argument?[39] What **specifically** got your goat? The other party may have said what they said to **deliberately** get you to fly off the handle on the premise that if you've reduced

---

[39] Such as, in the recent past, people were arguing that if gay marriage was allowed it would lead to people marrying their pets! This is an exaggerated slippery slope argument. A doesn't lead to Z, it might lead to B, an example in this case might be "if you allow gay marriage it might lead to legalizing polyamorous marriages." That's A -possibly leading to B. The false equivalence would be "if you allow gay sex, what's to stop people from incest or bestiality" - the answer being - NEITHER of those are the same as a healthy gay relationship or sexual encounter.

yourself to a screaming lunatic, you've lost that confrontation by default.

Take some time and identify each thing you can remember from the past which "set you off". Once you have that list, go over it and picture the conversation again. At the point you remember the other party saying what triggered your emotional response, imagine yourself practicing the pause and detachment exercise. Then picture what you would have said had you done that. This will reduce the chance of it happening again in the future (reduction) as you work to recall that new imagined reaction should someone use that tactic down the road.

Finally, reframe the remembered argument or hostile interaction. Picture yourself as the other party and saying (or doing) the things that transpired. Come up with a list of possible reasons why they did that? It can be for any hostile exchange, from remembered hours-long screaming matches to someone flipping you off on the highway. In the latter case, maybe they were late for an important meeting and you were driving slow in the passing lane, as you were not in a rush. Maybe you cut them off by accident? Put yourself in their shoes; see yourself getting upset over the slow driving numpty.

If you are a lead-foot driver yourself, try putting yourself in the slow driver's position. Maybe they've been in an accident recently and are terrified of another one or have gotten a speeding ticket not too long ago. They could just be trying to be a good driver. Maybe they are older, and their reflexes aren't as good as they once were, so they were driving slower to keep from getting into an accident. It could be any number of reasons.

In the case of the example regarding a screaming match - maybe the hostile party was stressed out about something else (their job, relationship, credit card debt, etc.)? Or perhaps they were simply passionately advocating their point of view. Reframe yourself as them, making their arguments and believing their position to be correct. You can also take it a step further and speculate that maybe **they** were insecure regarding their position on the topic you disagreed on. Or that they ego-identified too strongly with their own point of view and thus, your antagonism was viewed as personal when it was not.

If you yourself have been the person who so strongly identified with a position that you viewed other people attacking it as a personal affront, reframe the argument with the understanding that the other person had no real dog in that fight. It wasn't personal. Perceive it that way, and then re-imagine your response, knowing that it wasn't a personal attack on their part. You can also use this time to practice doing the detachment and delay exercise.

Exercise 4: Controlling Situations

A lot of the previous examples from exercise 3 are what you could call "unintentional". However, there are a number of reasons why someone might want to deliberately trick another person into losing control during an interaction. One reason is to make their opponent appear unhinged in order to damage their credibility. Another reason might be to get them to "slip up" and reveal information; suppressed feelings and desires can often come out in this way. Recognizing when this is occurring and responding calmly is key. This exercise is more about familiarizing yourself with these techniques and then applying the previous exercises as counters.

The first technique others might use against you is to put you in an unfamiliar environment, preferably with the ability to keep you there, in order to knock you off balance. Usually, it's a place with which you are unfamiliar and they are right at home. If it's a more public space, this can be countered by becoming familiar with it beforehand (if possible). If it's a more private space, your options are really just to leave as quickly as possible, insist on meeting on neutral ground, or to use the previous exercises to outlast whatever it is that they intend on achieving. Keep in mind, the suggestion to "meet on neutral ground" is often a ruse that you can use to get them on to ground, or in a space, with which you are at home. Cutting the interaction short and rescheduling is also a good tactic to assert control. If the location smells like a trap, it probably is a trap. Don't stay in it, or if you find yourself in it already, play dead emotionally if there is no polite fast way out of it.

The second technique they may use can be used with the first. It's when the other person arranges that you interact with them and their associates. This allows them to "gang up on you", taking turns to wear you down, increasing the likelihood that you will either agree to what they are selling, proposing, etc., or in the hope that coming at you from multiple directions will eventually result in you tripping up. Countering this involves having your own associates to hand, to offset this disadvantage, or in leaving as soon as possible. Conversely speaking, it can also be seen as a challenge to your emotional and responsive mastery. If you've become very good in one-on-one interactions, you may even turn this type of situation to your advantage, but if you recognize that intimidating you with numbers was the intention, get out of the situation.

Another method to be aware of is the infamous "close talker". They violate your personal space and attempt to dominate the situation (and specifically you) by towering over you or by pressing in too closely. This is easy enough to counter by maintaining space between you and them. If they constantly override this counter tactic, then I recommend leaving or confronting them with the fact that they are doing it.[40]

The next method of confrontational behavior comes in many guises. It can be a series of left-handed compliments or a negative comment disguised as an attempt at humor. They might attack some element or thing about you (appearance, shape, intelligence, etc.) in order to engender a response. All are an attempt to instill a sense of insecurity in you, which will then either throw you off balance, cause you to overreact or attack them, or to feel inadequate and as though you must please them. It's often possible in these situations, if you are quick witted enough, to turn it right back around on them. Measure for measure if you like. The second-best counter is to recognize it's happening and respond with dismissiveness: "Does <whatever it is> matter that much to you? I really don't put much stock in that." etc.

A crude and vulgar technique that appears in confrontations is a sudden burst of anger or a raised voice in an attempt to intimidate. It should immediately throw up red flags. They expect you to either be cowed or to respond in kind. This technique also portends that physical violence may not be far behind. Individuals who use this technique are often abusers. There is no better counter to this behavior than putting as much distance between you and them as possible or, if you're large enough, maintain your emotional control but meet fire with fire. Be careful though, as this could result in violence, and no matter what level of emotional control you have, if you find yourself in a fight, you've already lost.

The final technique is called "returning to the point". This is where, in conversation, your opposite number keeps returning to the beginning of the conversation and

---

[40] This one is often unintentional. There are many cultures where sitting/standing close and a lot of physical touching is "normal". Learn to discern when it's just cultural or when it's intentional before doing anything rash.

harping on whatever started the discussion/disagreement. It's as if nothing you said from that time to the present matted at all. "Master debaters" often use it. Just be cognizant that they are doing it. Counter it with "have you heard nothing that I've said <their name>?" If they don't give it up, just end the interaction. "This isn't going anywhere. Let's drop it / move on to the next point."

Exercise 5: Staying Between the Lines

This is an exercise in conformity. In other words, don't allow what you are feeling to either show on your face or, if it is socially understood that a reaction is normal, to only show what is expected. In this you must become an actor of sorts when you are with anyone else. Many do this naturally, others figure it out through experience. Regardless, it can be learned through a minimal amount of effort.

First, practice keeping your face relaxed. Any expression apart from a neutral one can betray what you are feeling. So, keep it limited to the occasional bland smile or the slightest frown. Keep your lips together and jaw relaxed. Teeth should be together but not clenched. Avoid grinding your teeth. Also, avoid showing your teeth: no broad grins or grimaces.

Once you have this pose mastered, expose yourself to something comedic. There is a ton of material online; expose yourself to as much as possible. If you don't have computer access, locate books of humorous anecdotes or jokes, and go through them. Resist the urge to laugh or show any other pronounced outward sign of gaiety. A slight smile is fine along with perhaps a minor tilt of the head. No more than that.

Next, expose yourself to the other stimuli which often engender an emotional response: horror, tragedy, sad music, etc. Though the horror film is often the best place to start, it can be used to master two types of reactions that you want to minimize - surprise and dread. It takes quite a bit of practice, mind you, to not have a surprised reaction when something comes at you unexpectedly, but as you would have already mastered pausing before responding to a verbal/emotional goading in the previous exercises you should have developed the habit of refraining from instantaneous reaction. Note: I don't think anyone is ever truly capable of NOT reacting to a genuine surprise. Jumping when you are startled is reflexive and beyond our control. However, the subsequent expressions beyond reflex ARE under your control, and the quicker regain your composure, the greater advantage you will have in any situation.

Along with expressive control, practice keeping a straight, but relaxed, posture when sitting or standing in the presence of others. Refrain from tensing your muscles or slouching. In high pressure situations, it may help to direct nervous strain. To assist this, you could use a hidden stress ball to squeeze as a last resort. Instead, I recommend focusing on your breathing and keeping it at a measured pace. If you used the counting method in the Trance chapter, employ it here.

After you've begun to control the physical aspects of emotion, practice speaking with an even and balanced tone. Your voice can easily betray what you are feeling, so avoid rises in tone, volume, or pitch. When speaking, keep your sentences short and to the point. Keep your pace of speech measured. Do not speak rapidly and risk stumbling over your sentences. Remember to pause before replying at all times. A short breath is a good measure of time for this; casually inhale and exhale through the nose first, and then respond.

Be aware of any verbal tics you might have. Don't fill gaps while talking with a lot of "ums" or "you knows" or "yeahs". Avoid upward inflection (allowing your voice to go up) at the end of any sentence that is NOT a question. If this is something you are unconsciously doing, work to drive it out of your speech. One means to accomplish this is to begin by record yourself having a conversation with someone. Play it back to yourself later, noting if you are doing any of the above, and work to cut it out.

Once you have mastered the above exercises, you should be able to maintain calm and composed in situations where many others would typically fly off the handle or come apart under the pressure. This will give you a decided advantage in stressful and confrontational situations. It will enable you to maintain control and even extend control over others down the road. Constant practice of these exercises is necessary. It will work to your advantage to and refresh your skills by periodically returning to them.

Joshua Wetzel

Chapter 6
Mental Control

How you think can be as important, or even more important, than what you think. This chapter will cover methods of establishing useful thinking habits and the use of those habits to assist in learning. It also will tie back into critical self-analysis and the practice of journaling yourself. The techniques you will be working with in the first half of this chapter are based on a methodology commonly known as NLP (Neuro-Linguistic Programming). There are a number of solid books on the topic of NLP, so feel free to use those to expand on the work you find here. In the second half of this chapter, we will go over the process of lucid dreaming and how that can be mastered and used to your advantage.

Part 1: Using NLP to control how you think

Neuro-Linguistic Programming (NLP) is a series of mindfulness techniques designed to both improve a person's control over how they think and increase their ability to effectively communicate with others. This is done through understanding how you frame your thinking, how you communicate (and by extension how other people think and communicate) and adjusting said thinking and communication to your advantage. This adjustment is accomplished by becoming aware of the sub modalities[41] and changing them, identifying your personal resources and exploiting them and finally by establishing future conditioning. I've broken this process down into a series of exercises below. The time frame for each depends

---

[41] **Sub modalities** are the fine distinctions we make within each representational system. They help us remember what we have seen, heard, felt, smelled and tasted.

on how readily you master them.

Part 1, Exercise 1: Identify how you (and those close to you) frame and process information

Our experiences, including all the information that comes into our mind, is filtered by a linguistic framework and then processed into types. Which set of words or descriptions that you use to communicate indicates which linguistic framework you use. Whether you group distinct stimuli together by similarity or by differences determines your preferred categorization type. Determining these should only take a few hours so allow one day for this exercise.[42]

Depending on your personal level of self consciousness, you may need to set up a recording device if you have one available to passively record what you are saying, e.g. if you know that you are paying attention to what you are saying will that change what you are saying and how? Otherwise just engage in several normal conversations with your acquaintances, or even total strangers, and try to pay attention to what words you use to frame the experience. This interaction can be verbal and in person or can be done digitally through texting or another means of messaging. You are looking for words that describe (or state the condition of) the things you are talking or texting about during that experience.

The conditional words you use will broadly fall into one of three categories: Visual, Auditory or Kinesthetic (See Table 1 / page 40 "Mindworks"). Nearly everyone uses one of these three filters when processing information. For this exercise, identify which set you primarily use. That's it. You now know your linguistic framework for

---

[42] It's ok to take a couple of days depending on how much social interaction you engage in.

interacting with the world.

> Table 1:
>
> Visual - see / look / imagine / eye-to-eye / can you see what i'm saying? / sights / light / clear / murky / glaring / focus / glimpse / the sight of / shadow(s) / blurry / blank / blind
>
> Auditory - hear / listen / sound / tell-yourself / can you hear what i'm saying? / blaring / loud / resonant / good ear / booming / tune in or out / echo / whisper / deaf / silence / pitch / tone
>
> Kinesthetic - feel, touch, grasp, place yourself in my shoes, balance, how does that make you fee? / solid / hard / sharp / smooth / punch / rough / brush off / mute

Continue to observe yourself interacting with other people now that you know your linguistic framework. Step 2 of this exercise is to determine how you process the information that you have framed. Determine whether you group things by how much they are "like" each other or if you understand their relationships by how much one thing "differs" from another. Understand that this is normally a totally unconscious process. One type of process or framework is not better or worse than any other. It's simply a matter of becoming aware of which one you use.

Indications of which process you use (similarity or difference) might include, but are not limited to, some of the example phrases below:

"That was a great x, it was just like the time..." (sameness)

"It was fine, except the part about x could have been better..." (difference)

<come back and add a few more>

Once you have your process and framework well in hand, it's time to move on to the next exercise. This will involve manipulating the information and experiences that you have come to possess in a way which will assist you going forward. In essence, it's time to play with your past and adjust it to benefit you. You remember the past via your preferred framework and process. By making adjustments to them you will turn your own experiences into a resource or, if the experience was negative, reduce its hampering impact.

Part 1, Exercise 2: Manipulating Memory

We live in the bubble of the present. Not only is the future changeable, but the past is as well.[43] Neuroscientists have known for some time, that our memories are extremely fallible, changeable, and thus, rewritable. This can be used to adjust memories. Memories that were painful or embarrassing or frightening, i.e. memories that haunt us or hamper our ability to take on new challenges and goals, can have their power to hinder us taken away. Conversely speaking, pleasant memories of happy events, encounters, successes, triumphs, etc. can be empowered. Subsequently, this also grants us the ability to access those positive characteristics and feelings as resources later, on demand, when needed.

Through this exercise, you will take a selection of memories (both positive and negative) and adjust them in a fairly straightforward manner.

Exercise 2a: Take a negative memory, like when you failed to meet the expectations of a group of people. Maybe you were in a play and forgot your lines on stage, or you were giving a presentation that went poorly. Perhaps you were called on in class and got the wrong answer or couldn't answer a question in front of the other students and were laughed at. We've all had experiences like these (or much,

---

[43] '"It's a poor sort of memory that only works backwards," the Queen remarked. "What sort of things do YOU remember best?" Alice ventured to ask. "Oh, things that happened the week after next," the Queen replied in a careless tone'. - Lewis Carroll, Alice in Wonderland

much worse).

Return to that memory. Picture it with as much detail as you can: the feelings, what was said (or as much of what was said as you can remember), the lighting of the room, the color of the walls, the sounds that people around you were making, the temperature, etc. Much of how you recall it will depend on the type of framing that you use. If you use a visual framework, the lights and colors and images will dominate. If you use auditory, it will be the sounds. If you're kinesthetic, it will be how you felt (Though obviously regardless of your framing I presume you felt bad at the time).

Once you have it remembered as best you can play it back from the beginning but turn off the colors of the room, put everything in grayscale. Black and white. Like an old-time movie or TV show. As it continues, and you recall your experience of that shitty time, reduce the volume of any noise that occurred, if there was laughter directed at you, muffle it, recall the sound of low-grade canned laughter used on recorded tv comedies. Replace what you remember with that. Play it back again, this time with everything smaller, still in black and white, far away, like an old tiny TV, quiet, barely there. Repeat at that level one more time and then move on to the next negative memory.

You should do this for at least three negative memories. However, you can also repeat this for every bad memory or experience that you have had. The goal here is not to try and force yourself to forget them. Nor erase them. Nor suppress them. Even bad memories teach us things. In fact, what we learned from them at the time is the thing we want to keep. What we are doing through this exercise is keeping the lesson learned, whatever that may have been, but robbing the memory of the force of paralyzing impact.

Exercise 2b: This is almost the reverse of the above with a few additions. Recall at least three positive memories where you won something, a game or competition, or scored really well on a test, or did really well at making something, whether it was written, musical or physical, doesn't matter. Again, you don't have to limit yourself to three but for the purpose of this exercise this is the minimum. They don't have to involve the praise of others these memories, you may have done something amazing with no recognition, regardless of that, you know that you did it and you did it WELL. That still counts.[44]

Recall each of these memories, one at a time, to the best of your ability. In addition to recalling them you are also going to journal them. Keep a record of them. This record should be added to whenever your recall additional positive memories. This will aid in the next exercise.

As with exercise 2a try and remember as much as possible about the experience. What were the sights, the sounds, the noise (or lack thereof) the smells, etc. Try and remember what was said (if it was primarily verbal). Once you have a good idea of the memory in your minds eye bring it closer to your mental perspective. Make the colors brighter, the sounds a bit louder (but not overwhelmingly loud). Remember it again, i.e. play it through in your memory in high-def as it were. Determine what it was about what you were doing that was a positive reflection on you. Did you score well on a test? Did you perform well/win a game? Did you tell a hilarious joke or perform a really funny prank? Did you make something really well? Attempt to feel again what you felt then but with the volume / brightness and feeling of joy/success/happiness turned up.

---

[44] I should add, don't be afraid to reach out to people that have known you for a long time if this one seems to be a stumper. Sometimes (not all the time but sometimes) relatives and friends can be a kick to recall good things about us that we've forgotten...though really, after some serious self reflection you should be able to recall good events in your life yourself, but I thought I would throw that out there.

Part 1, Exercise 3: Identify your Resources. Name them.

One postulate of NLP for the practitioner is this: "You already have all the resources you will ever need."[45] The trick is determining what those are and using them to your advantage on demand. It's no good coming up with a list of personal resources, i.e. abilities and talents and aptitudes, if when you need them they are unavailable or blocked off.

Go over the journal entries from exercise 2b. In each success or good memory there is, ideally, something about you that made it possible. Take each of these and name them. Were you creative? Quick? (Physically or mentally), Knowledgeable? Well rehearsed? Prepared? Funny? Patient? Calm and confident under stress? Exacting? Crafty? Cunning? Each and every one of these is a personal resource of yours that you can draw on at will. But before drawing on it, you have to identify it. Use the memories of exercise 2b to find your list of internal resources. Name each one. Use this list for the next exercise.

Part 1, Exercise 4: Anchoring of Resources and their Exploitation.

It's one thing to know what resources you possess in terms of natural aptitudes and innate talent. It's another matter entirely to be able to draw upon those resources at will in circumstances that require them. Fortunately, the ability to do so can be learned. The process of being able to call upon your resources at will is called anchoring.

Anchoring is a process of making a reaction automatic. It can occur naturally, such as when we constantly get exposed to performing an expected response to a stimulus

---

[45] Mindworks - Anne Linden

and do so without thinking. Such as the automatic "Good Morning" or "Hello" to a passing greeting. Or the obligatory "Bless you!" to a sneeze. The whole genre of martial arts is, in fact, based on automatic reflexive responses to various acts of physical aggression.

The ultimate example, trope, or cited instance of the learned response is, of course, Pavlov's dog. Ring the bell, put the food down, dog salivates and eats. Ring the bell, put the food down, dog salivates and eats. Ring the bell, no food, but the dog still salivates. The response to the food (salivation) is transferred from seeing the food to hearing the bell (the anchor). People can be trained to do much the same thing and you can train yourself to create your own anchors. In this case to your inner resources.

Step 1: First determine what your anchor is. It should be a simple physical gesture; such as pressing your thumb and another finger together on your dominant hand.[46] Or resting your chin on your hand, your hand being gently closed in a fist. Or resting your hand on your knee. Or crossing your arms. The only real qualifier is that it should be a distinct but subtle gesture.

Step 2: Take one of the resources identified from the previous exercise. Again, go over the memory in which the resource played a role in as much detail as possible. Make the memory as vivid as possible. Remember it in the clearest details. At the point at which your talent/resource is evident during the memory create your anchor. Hold the anchor while you feel what you felt at the time of the memory and hold it for 10 to 12 seconds.

Step 3: Release the anchor gesture and take several deep

---

[46] And surprise, surprise between two hands you can easily anchor 8 separate resources or more.

breaths. Look around for about 15 seconds and then repeat Step 2 four more times.

Step 4: After you have done the fifth time take a short break and think on other things. After about a minute or two make your anchor gesture - the feelings you associate with the anchor should come flooding back.

That's it, you've created an anchor for that resource that you can call upon in an upcoming situation. You can repeat this exercise to create anchors to all the inner resources that you possess with a unique gesture for each resource/anchor. Tools now ready to be used in whatever circumstance calls for them.

Part 1, Exercise 5: Future Conditioning (optional)

While it's good to be able to access your resources through anchoring them, and thus be able to call them up at a moment's notice with your anchor, it's even better to have them ready in advance of known situations in which a particular resource will come in handy. The ability to transfer the anchor to an upcoming encounter is known in NLP as "future conditioning" and it is the last exercise in this Section of the book on NLP.[47]

Picture, if you will, an upcoming encounter that you know will be fraught with difficulty. Perhaps it's a meeting with a difficult client or your boss or with a relative that stresses you out. If you are familiar with the setting or the person, i.e. you recognize it or them, you can anchor a resource to them so that it will activate when you see them or find yourself in the place of the encounter.

Let's say the resource that you have anchored is confidence and the situation is an upcoming meeting with

---

[47] NLP will come up in Section 2 as well.

your boss during your review. Close your eyes and picture the face of your boss. Now while picturing their mug perform the gesture associated with your anchor for confidence. Hold that for 5 seconds then open your eyes and release your gesture. Repeat this process 2 or 3 more times. Now for the 4th time simply close your eyes and picture the face of your boss. Your resource should activate. You have now transferred that anchor to their face and the resource of confidence will manifest when you see them in person.

A couple of concluding notes: Each anchor should have its own unique gesture. Do NOT use the same gesture for multiple anchors - it will muddle the anchoring process and dilute the force of the resources. Also be aware that while an anchored resource may help in a difficult situation it may get overwhelmed by a disastrous situation. This is not to say that it might not still come in handy, but keep in mind it's a resource - not a silver bullet. An oar is a resource that will always allow you to row a boat, but its effectiveness is different during a bit of rough weather on the one hand and a typhoon on the other.

Part 2: Lucid Dreaming

Control of your thinking process can also be extended to the realm of dreams. Lucid dreaming, i.e. the obtaining of conscious awareness while in the dreaming state and gaining control of the dream itself is the final set of exercises in the realm of mental control. It can be used in a number of ways once mastered. On the one hand, it can be used as a tool of extending perception - i.e. dream divination. On the other hand it can be used to assist in the mastery of mundane skills by providing an optimal <venue?> to create a positive feedback loop for a personal talent that you possess.

Part 2, Exercise 0: Get enough sleep

Every subsequent step in this part of the chapter will not be possible if you do not get enough sleep. Which is why, before you even start, work on getting enough sleep. How much is enough depends a lot on your sleep personality type. Over the years I've found that most people fall into one of three categories which I will label type A, type B and type C. None of these types are inherently better or worse than the other and there is no benefit being one type over the other. That being said, which type you are determines how much sleep you need to be able to master lucid dreaming.

Type A is the most common type and they typically sleep between 7 and 8 hours a night. As will all sleepers yes, they do wake up for brief moments of time during the night but generally fall back to sleep without remembering those interruptions. As they are the majority of people this is why most sleep experts recommend a 7 to 8 hour sleep schedule as it covers the greatest number of people.

Type B is less common but is often as numerous as the first (though some don't recognize it and think they are just shitty "A" or "C" type sleepers). Type B sleepers fall asleep early in the evening, sleep[48] for three to four hours, wake up for anywhere from 1 to 3 hours in the middle of the night, then fall back asleep again for another 3 to four hours of sleep.

Type C is the least common. These are people who get by on 4 to 5 hours of sleep a night, every night. For them even this brief stint is enough to remember their dreams and be well rested. Some Type B sleepers sometimes think that they are Type C but they are not, nor are they

---

[48] Early in the evening is relative. I've seen some B type sleepers fall asleep in the afternoon, get up in the evening and stay up until 3 or 4 in the morning and then go back to sleep and get up again around 9 or 10 AM. It's all relative to when your first sleep cycle is if you are a B type sleeper.

insomniacs, they are just not getting their second sleep cycle in and are hurting for it.

As a general rule Type A sleepers recall their dreams only at the end of sleep, the same for Type C. Type B sleepers tend to recall both at the end of sleep cycle 1 and sleep cycle 2. All types may awaken and recall a dream at any point during the night but the above is mostly true for most dreamers. Regardless of which type you are, try to get the amount of sleep that best suits your type. This will increase the probability of you having good dream recall and being able to jot your dreams down.

Part 2, Exercise 1: Dream Journaling

Lucid Dreaming is dependent on dream recall. Dream recall is dependent on the dreamer consistently remembering their dreams. The way to increase your dream recall and make the ability to do so on a regular basis a reality, is by dream journaling. The way you record your dreams is up to you. Most prefer to keep a notepad by the side of the bed and write down what they dreamed. Others have a laptop or tablet which can be quickly accessed. Some have used audio recordings and subsequent transcription to track their dreams. Pick a method that works best for you and stick with it.[49]

Record every dream you can. Most find that as they are recording the last dream of the night other, earlier dreams will sometimes come back to them. Record as much as you can. Pay attention to what you saw, how you felt, who you encountered, what you encountered, etc. Keep your dream journal separate from any other types of journals you might be keeping as it can often get quite wordy and needs thus to be a thing apart.

---

[49] And yes, if you pick one method and it doesn't work well, try another one until you find the one that works best for you.

Part 2, Exercise 2: Identifying and Cataloging Dream Signs & and asking, "is this a dream?"

As you start to consistently recall and record your dreams, probably after two or three weeks of performing Exercise 1, begin looking for what is known as "dream signs" - i.e. indications that you, in fact dreaming. Some dream signs are often specific to the individual but there are others that are very often shared, and common among all or most dreamers. Here are a few examples from my own dreams:

A book in which what is written keeps changing or which is impossible to read. An old time clock with an odd number of hands (i.e. just one, or four, etc) or with an odd number of hours (13, 14, etc). A digital clock whose face is unreadable or for which the time rapidly changes. Something flying which shouldn't be, including yourself. Someone you once knew but never see anymore like a long lost friend or a dead relative or even a dead pet. A house or apartment that you used to live in but haven't for ages. These (and many others) can be dream signs.

The dream signs purpose, for us, is that it is a giveaway that you are dreaming and it can thus be used to trigger a lucid dream - i.e. when you recognize the dream, ask yourself "Is this a dream?" and you may thus find that yes, yes it is and congratulations, you have obtained lucidity in that dream.

Getting into the habit of asking "is this a dream?" to yourself shouldn't be confined to dreaming. It's something that you should get in the habit of asking yourself several times throughout the day or when something peculiar or unexpected happens - i.e. like when you run into that long lost acquaintance, former coworker, friend or partner unexpectedly. Getting into the habit of questioning reality while awake will increase the likelihood of remembering to do so while dreaming and thus triggering a lucid dream.

Part 2, Exercise 3: Staying dreaming and lucid

A major challenge experienced by many lucid dreamers is retaining lucidity after achieving it. Too often the dreamer either wakes up right away or the dream goes back to being non-lucid very quickly. Luckily there are some techniques that other lucid dreams have discovered to stay in that lucid state for longer periods of time. A couple of methods are listed below.

The first method is by concentrating on another sense rather than vision within the lucid dream. Touch something in the dream, try to smell something, try to listen to whatever noises, voices or music might be occurring. Or if you are very visually cued try focusing your sight on something in the dream, an object or the ground for example. Looking at your hands or body in general can also help stabilize the lucid dreaming state - basically, attention is directed at a known and unchanging object or part of the self.

The second method is to spin like a top (or dervish or whatever works) in the dream state. Throw out your dream arms before the dream state fades and spin. Remind yourself while doing it that the next thing you see will be another dream. Should you think you have failed to remain sleeping, i.e. it's not uncommon to dream that you have awakened and all the while you are still dreaming. Have something indisputably real to check in your bedroom - a digital clock or a book by the bed are good examples - if you can't read the face of the clock because the numbers are all goofy or changing, then you are still dreaming. The same goes for a book by the bed - if you pick it up and can't read it because the text keeps changing, you are still dreaming and can continue with the lucid dreaming process.

***

Part 2, Exercise 4: I'm lucid dreaming, now what?

Once you have mastered the ability to lucid dream on a fairly regular basis the obvious question is "now what?" - What can I use this newfound ability to accomplish? How can I use it to improve my current situation? Is it more than just a trick of the mind? Can it be used for magic? Absolutely. This exercise will cover some of the uses for lucid dreaming that the practitioner can exploit to their advantage.

The first use of lucid dreaming is creative problem solving. Before you go to bed pick a problem that you would like to dream the solution to. It can be anything, large or small like "What career should I pursue?" or "How do I accomplish 'x' goal?" Write down the question and memorize it. As you fall asleep repeat the question in your mind while having the intention to become lucid. When you become lucid in the dream ask the question again in the lucid dreaming state. Continue the dream. It may be necessary to use the techniques to retain lucidity above. Upon awakening immediately record the solution. Lucid dreams are like any other dream, they can fade just as quickly so don't lose the information obtained.

Another use for lucid dreaming is skill mastery. For example, if you are about to engage in learning something new like an instrument or are currently learning how to play one. Or you are going to be learning how to build something or create something, etc. Write down what you intend to practice doing (if you have the opportunity to watch an expert at whatever it is during the day do so too). The intention should be clearly worded like: "I will practice violin in my dream." or "I will build the new deck for my house in my dream." etc., memorize what you wrote down. As with the previous example repeat it silently to yourself as you fall asleep with the intention to lucid dream. You can even see yourself doing it, a conscious visualization, as you fall asleep as a dry run. But regardless, focus on what it is and the intention to lucid dream doing it. When you become lucid in the dream execute the activity in the dream state. Picture yourself doing it better than you, or anyone else, ever has. You can write down what you experienced/felt but unlike the first use listed above, this recording is optional.

The third use of lucid dreaming is the extension of perception. A dream state is, in and of itself, a trance state and the same goes for a lucid dreaming state. Encode your intention into a mantra. Recite that mantra to yourself as you fall asleep combined with the intention of lucid dreaming. When you become lucid in the dream search out the answer. Upon waking - immediately write down the answer that you sought. Note: Unlike with the first use above it is possible to get an answer to the divination without obtaining lucidity. It may come naturally in the dream state in symbolic form - regardless, record the contents of the first dream that you recall upon waking lucid or not.

Chapter 7
Group Magick: It Kind of Sucks

To be certain, group magick has its uses. It can be used to create a shared mythology and history for any collection of individuals who participate in it. It can foster social cohesion and a sense of belonging, especially in the performance of initiations. Hell, it creates group identity and says "this is us" when done correctly. The best utilization of group magick is to teach and to share methods and ideas; this is its greatest value in my opinion, and I will cover its use briefly.

Social groups are extremely important to the toxick magician. People are your most important resource, and true isolation can ultimately only lead to failure. So being in a group that does magick isn't a waste of time. In fact, it's optimal to belong to one (just not one that is a collection of toxick magicians). Fortunately, there are all sorts of flavors of occult practitioners out there for you to associate with. They range from those who accept anyone with a pulse, up to those who weed out 97% of applicants. So pick one that appeals to you and join.

In whatever organization you join, you can practice your social skills and learn techniques and approaches to doing magick that you normally would not have come across on your own. This demonstrates the teaching value that groups have. In any group, there are always members that have the desire to teach and instruct. Whether that is out of genuine desire to share knowledge or as a method of controlling others by leading them in ritual (imparting the notion that that person is, by default, the "leader"), the sharing of knowledge occurs nonetheless.

That being said, be wary of those who take teaching to the extreme, likening themselves to a guru. Odds are they want less to teach and more to take your money or get in your pants. When considering various groups to join, do your homework first. It's a thin line between a group that adds value to your life and a cult that, once in, you can't get out of without a lot of effort and pain. Be particularly gun shy of smaller groups centered around one charismatic individual. That way shares the likes of Charles Manson and his "family", to name just one example.

How can you tell a cult from an organization? One simple way is to ask what happens to those that join and, more importantly, what happens to those that leave. Groups that isolate the individual from their natural family should immediately raise the alarm. Those that attempt to kill or severely harm those who become apostates are also to be avoided. I would also add groups to this list that recruit aggressively. If they want you, that's one thing. If they want you, your partner, and your entire extended family – that's no good; Run for the hills.

The sense of belonging (the "one of us" value) shouldn't be overlooked when it comes to any group either. Social contacts established in this way can be a literal lifeline to provide help when you need it, job opportunities, dating possibilities, a shoulder to cry on, people on your side when others attempt to hurt you, and much more. The value is clear and obvious.

This is all well and good but remember to keep a sense of detachment. Don't get lost in whatever group you involve yourself in. Ultimately, they are only a resource to be exploited. An experienced toxick magician will know that any group, as such, is plug and play; any group will do. The one you happen to choose is arbitrary. If you lose your focus, the group will ultimately use you more than you use them. While a quid-pro-quo is fine under most circumstances, one must be mindful of the balance between you using them and them using you. When it tilts

Joshua Wetzel

towards their advantage, it's time to consider getting out.

Groups are also not advantageous when it comes to doing magick. Peter Carroll once wrote, "The effects of a number of persons conjuring simultaneously or sequentially for a common objective never exceeds the best result that any one of them might achieve ."[50] It stands to reason, and experience will bear this out, that the most effective method of magick is performed by the least number of skilled participants: ideally, one person working alone. The more people involved, the lower the probability of success.

Each and every individual obtains a state of ekstasis at their own pace. Some may take a few dozen minutes (or even less), while others are best off banging away for a few hours. In any given ritual some people will have peaked early, some at the desired time of executing whatever the intention was, while some will not even be close. The entire group's effort is dragged down by the effectiveness of the least effective individual, negatively impacting the whole. The end result being a flop for everyone in terms of ritual outcome.

The fact of the matter is, if you're not using a group ritual to learn or as an aspect of social engineering, you might as well be flushing your intentions down the toilet for all the good it's doing you. The manipulation of your reality cannot be effectively steered with the intentions of others. It's like multiple people trying to drive the same car at once, each with a different destination in mind. Hell, even if everyone has the same destination, the metaphor holds; a car only needs one driver. Adding any more just invites failure.

Generally speaking, the person leading the ritual, and perhaps a few of their closest associates, are the only ones who have a vested interest in the ritual's outcome.

[50] "Liber Kaos" p. 48

Everyone else participating is just a drag on the probability of success. Overall, stick to doing rituals with as few people as possible, or you and your partner (if you're inclined to do something like tantra[51]), but preferably just yourself.

In this way, you maximize the probability of success. Exploit whatever group or groups you associate with for their ability to teach you new things, as a resource in times of trouble, or as a way of practicing manipulation. Don't rely on them for magical success. For that, you're on your own.

---

[51] Tantra, sex magick for people who have the time to waste 8 hours at a go fucking.

Chapter 8
Magick without Banishing (Integrated Magick)

The practitioner needs to divorce themselves from the notion that any space is distinctly mundane or distinctly magical. The manifestation of one's will, even if its implementation involves the use of ekstatic or trance states, should be viewed and internalized as being a natural and an organic part of life. It must be perceived as something which is a subset of a multilayered approach to achieving one's goals. Don't look at it as an extreme or bizarre avenue taken only when one is desperate, but as another road that reaches the same destination.

Too often the traditional occultist lives in a bubble by dressing in silly robes in ill lit rooms, cloyed with incense, and playing with symbolic (and often useless) paraphernalia. In chaos magic rituals in particular there is a formulaic construction which is used in the vast majority of rites that have been created to date: A banishing of some variety (I.A.O., Star Ruby, G.P.R. etc.), followed by "a statement of intent," the body of the ritual in one or more parts, and concluded with another banishing. All of which reinforces the idea that what is happening isn't "real".

Other groups are even worse. Their "magick" is little better than religion. They just go through the motions of a ritual. It's not magick; it's a pathetic pantomime of it — reading someone else's words off a page, enacting someone else's creation. They might as well be in a church and dropping a dollar in the collection plate when they're done. Nothing could be farther from actually DOING magick.

While I can frankly see why this is done on one level — the magician is theoretically saying to themselves and their fellow participants, "I am going beyond the mundane into the magical, which gives the effort to reach this goal a special force and/or meaning" — on another level, what they are unfortunately saying is, "I can't accomplish my goal(s) through the use of my intellect, my ability to carry out a plan, networking with others, or through sheer hard work. I lack those options," and, "This part of my life is cut off from the rest of my life."

I would also argue that quite a number of occultists are, in fact, properly opening up the mundane avenues of manifestation. Their magical work is just to give their effort an extra push to succeed. There's no denying that. Unfortunately, I fear that they are in the minority. The majority are performing their magick in the hope that the rite itself will substitute the need to do any actual work on their part. One should be keen to not fall into the latter group.

In regards to the former group (those who aren't relying on a well performed ritual to get the results they seek), my contention is that they are sabotaging themselves with the implication stated above that "This part of my life is cut off from the rest of my life" when they perform a banishing. They also undermine themselves when they utter a statement of intent, though that is a form of sabotage of another kind. Both should be assiduously avoided.

So then, how should one approach doing a ritual? How would one have it be part of one's life and not divorce it in a symbolic sense? Easy. It's simply added onto the end of your daily practice established in chapter 2. After a solid meditation, launch into whatever ritual you were planning to perform. You can exploit the trance state obtained during the meditation or you can ramp yourself up into an ecstatic state to fire off your intention. Either way, the magick you do will be an element of your life similar to your daily meditation, not something psychologically distinct from what you are already doing.

You need no special robes, wands, incense, or altar. To a toxick magician, their magick is already part of their reality. It can be performed anywhere and at any time. When needed, just do it. It takes only a minute to encode most intentions, and once you have mastered getting into a variety of ekstatic states, they are there on demand. With that in mind, it does pay to continue following the recommendations about planning ahead and being proactive. It's never good to be in a reactive frame all the time. If you find yourself always responding to the actions of others, rather than directing the course of events, it might be time to step back from whatever group or project you are part of in order to reassert control.

Constantly keep magick as an integrated part of your existence. Have it be as natural as spending money or persuading someone to get what you want. The desired magical result will flow seamlessly into your reality along the avenues of manifestation that you have already opened up for it.[52] Just as anything else that you work for. The only difference being that you've used the tool of magick to assist in achieving it, ensuring success, and providing yourself with an edge. Leave the banishings to the magical dilettantes and amateurs.

---

[52] See chapter 4 in this section.

Chapter 9
Agents and Egregores

Agents, commonly known as "Servitors," are an alternative method for the extension of the practitioner's will. Unlike a sigil (charged with a single instance of ekstasis and then destroyed), agents are long term, periodically recharged, detached, and semi-autonomous elements of your will. They are deployed when circumstances call for a continuous reinforcement of your intention as opposed to a "one and done" situation. For example, maybe instead of a new partner, you wish to be constantly attracting new partners so that you have a better chance of finding the person (or persons) that works best for you, or you might be faced with a chronic or long-term medical condition. In such a situation, a one-off attempt at magical healing would not suffice. Another situation might be that you desire more than one financial or job opportunity or contract. All of these and more might call for creating and maintaining an agent.

Egregores, on the other hand, are created by a group of individuals working together over a prolonged, open-ended period of time. Egregores are more commonly known as totems, gods, deities, archetypes or some other variety of spirit. They are often tied to a specific location; a mountain, river, forest, star, or a specific phenomenon; lightning, wind, rain, earthquakes, the dawn, death, sex, war, wealth, etc. Over the millennia, people have come to believe that by directing worship and entreaties to the personification of these locations or phenomenon they could reap some kind of benefit or avoid some calamity.

In the case of agents, your approach should be to create them for a single purpose, recharge them as necessary, and then decommission them when they are no longer needed. In the case of egregores, the magician seeks to hijack the energy directed at the egregore for their own use. I will go over examples of both in the exercises below. I will also touch on daemons/demons and the spirits of the dead, as they fall between the two categories of agents and egregores in many respects. As such, they are not optimal for use by you[53] for getting what you want, but as they are frequently encountered in the occult, they deserve a mention.

Part 1: Agents

The first step in the creation of an Agent is a clear and succinct intention along with a name for the agent. Figure out what you want and phrase it in a clear and direct manner. Avoid any form of circumspection or innuendo, e.g. if you goal is to attract multiple sexual partners don't state, "It is my will to create an agent to attract loving individuals to me" — that's not what you *really* want, so don't use it. Instead, use, "It is my will to create an agent to attract new sexual partners." The second step is to consider what elements or abilities the agent should possess which would aid it in assisting to achieve your results. These will be incorporated into the mental image of the agent: it's non-corporeal form, i.e. how you perceive it in your mind's eye. Step three is the creation of a physical base for the Agent. The physical base serves three purposes — a location to direct a periodic recharge to keep it energized, a reminder to yourself that the agent is active, and something to be destroyed when the agent is decommissioned. Step four is determining what type of ekstasis state you will use to charge the Agent. While any type can be used, I've found[54] that it makes sense to match

---

[53] Or anyone else really.
[54] And others have come to this conclusion. I wasn't the first, just wanted to make that clear.

the type of ekstasis to the intention when possible, e.g. if the function of the Agent is sexual then the ekstasis used should be sexual. Of course some intentions don't have an exact ekstatic match, so you can be flexible. Finally, determine how long the Agent will be in effect. A month, 3 months, a year, longer? Try to have an end date in mind. Do not allow Agents to be open-ended. Have a decommission date in mind before you start. I'll go over all the steps below in more detail and give examples.

Part 1, Step 1: Come up with an intention and a name.

The most common uses for Agents are (but are not limited to): protection of self or others, healing[55], finding lost items, extension of perception (usually through dreams and visions), gaining wealth/money, or attracting sexual/romantic partners. Regardless of what it will be used for, the intention should be clear and focus on a single purpose. If you have more than one objective or function in mind, create separate Agents for each of them rather than trying to use one for many or reusing an Agent over and over again. I will provide examples below of Agent creation for 3 separate agents — one for magical protection against misfortune, one for attracting wealth, and one for finding lost items. Obviously with slight modifications, Agent type 1 could be modified to provide healing, Agent type 2 could be modified to attract a sexual partner, and Agent type 3 could be modified to answer divinatory questions.

The creation of the intention is simple but comes in two parts. One is reusable, and the other is customized to the agent's specific function. For all three examples, the first

---

[55] Standard disclaimer that creating an agent to deal with a chronic health issue is not a substitute for seeking professional medical care from a professional. Use in conjunction with, NOT as a replacement for.

part is to take the following statement—I will into existence an agent—and turn it into a mantra via duplicate letter elimination and rearrangement as described in Section 1. Viz:

I will into existence an agent
I WIL NTO EXSTC AG
CLETOW GANIXS

Once that is done, the same process is conducted for the specific purview of the agent. Agent 1 being "For magical protection", Agent 2 being "For attracting wealth", Agent 3 being "For always finding lost items." The second is then combined with the first (see below).

For magical protection
FOR MAGICL PTEN
PROF CLAG NETIM

For attracting wealth
FOR ATCING WELH
GRANI CLEFT WOH

For always finding lost items
FOR ALWYS INDG T EM
DETIF WORN LYS GAM

Intention creation for Agent 1 result:
Cletow Ganixs Prof Clag Netim

Intention creation for Agent 2 result:
Cletow Ganixs Grani Cleft Woh

Intention creation for Agent 3 result:
Cletow Ganixs Detif Worn Lys Gam

Now we just need to come up with a name, and if you saw how I chose to rearrange the residual letters, you might be able to spot where I was going with this part. Looking at what resulted, I'm going with "Professor

Clag" for Agent 1, "Granny Woh" for Agent 2 and "Detective Worn" for Agent 3: names which came out of the process of rearranging the letters to make the sigil. It's simple, direct, and just about any intention might yield such a title/name combination that jumps out at you.

If, however, the name doesn't jump out at you, there are several ways to divine it. The first is to take the completed intention/creation phrase and perform a Trance exercise using sound concentration as described in Section 1. Alternatively, you can take the completed intention and perform a glossolalia Ekstasis exercise to get the name. A final option is to use the completed intention and perform a lucid dreaming session in which the name is produced. However it's obtained you will now have the intention and name sorted out and can move on to Step 2.

Part 1, Step 2: Elements and Abilities

Now that you have an intention and a name, it's time to come up with what attributes the Agent will possess. For example, an Agent that's primary role is finding things might be given a large eye or eyes, while an Agent that is defending you magically would possess a shield of some sort, and Agent that is attracting something might have a large magnet. These will be a primary attribute of each, and Agents can possess multiple attributes. All of them should, however, be in line with the Agent's function.

In my above example, "Professor Clag" will have a large shield, "Granny Woh" will have a large magnet, and "Detetive Worn" will possess a large Sherlock Holmes style magnifying glass. See the image on the next page:

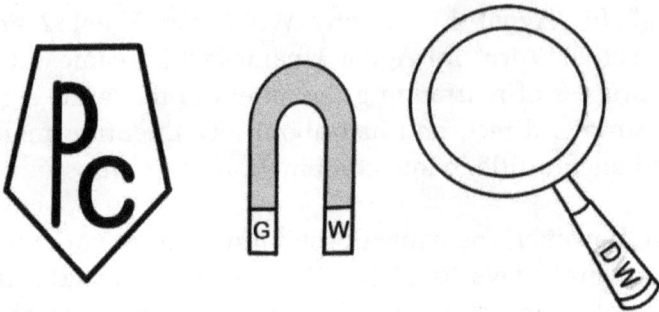

The rest of the mental image of the Agent is up to you—they can be as anthropomorphic, theriomorphic[56], or as abstract as you like—it's your agent, imagine it as you will. They should be recognizable as themselves, i.e. when you look at the image that you have created, you know without thinking that, "Aha, that is Agent x," and you know what it's for. I typically draw shapes around the main attribute with sub-attributes for other minor abilities that I would like the Agent to possess—like speed, strength, or flight.

Part 1, Step 3: Creation of the Physical Base

Now that you have an image or idea of what the Agent will look like, create a physical base for it. This will allow you to interact with the Agent. The main types of interactions are, of course, the initial charging and tasking of the Agent (see step 4), additional instructions, additional charging, and terminating through decommissioning. The Agent can be drawn on paper as seen above, molded into clay, carved into wood, etched into metal, baked into bread, etc. Really just about any physical medium will do. The only exception being to avoid something like a tattoo of the Agent—it's meant to be temporary and disposable, not permanent. Save your attachments for actual people. Once

---

[56] As human shaped or as animal shaped respectively.

you have determined your physical base, create the Agent.

Part 1, Step 4: Determine Ekstasis, Link, and Charge Agent

Pick an Ekstatis from Section 1, Chapter 3 and use it to work yourself up into that state. During this process you can chant the intention from Step 1 above, or you can simply have it running through your mind. At the height/peak of Ekstasis, visualize the Agent coming forth from you and into the physical base that you created in Step 3. When you reach this point you can, optionally, anoint the physical base with a bodily fluid (blood[57], spit, semen/vaginal fluid) as a way of sealing the link of the Agent to you. This process can be repeated whenever you feel you need to recharge the Agent. Typically, this is done once a month or at the same point in a lunar cycle. If you want, it can be as frequent as once a week or as infrequent as you desire, but don't expect fantastic results from a seldom charged Agent.

Part 1, Step 5: Decommission Agent

That's basically about it—place the physical base of the Agent in a safe, secure location. Take it out whenever you want to specifically direct it or recharge it. Otherwise, it should act autonomously until decommissioned. Generally, you decommission an Agent at a pre-arranged time, either after it has completed its task or after a set period. I recommend not keeping an Agent active for any more than a year, and a shorter period of time than even that is preferable.

Once you have reached that point, you simply destroy

---

[57] The best way to use blood in this manner is to prick your finger with a lancet - lancets are available either on the shelf or over the counter at pharmacies everywhere and very cheep.

Joshua Wetzel

the physical base of the agent and visualize it dissolving in your mind's eye. Alternatively, you can visualize it being reabsorbed into yourself. Either way, destroy the physical base. Burn it, smash it, eat it; the method does not matter so long as the base is destroyed and the Agent pictured dissolved. Agents, used in concert with Sigils and Avenues of Manifestation, can be highly effective.

Part 2: Egregores

Throughout human history our species has believed in supernatural entities. To early humanity these beings were responsible for creating the universe, causing storms, disease, birth, death, earthquakes, creating fire, etc., and they were therefore worthy of being worshiped. Typically called "gods," these constructs would be sacrificed to, prayed at, pleaded with, and generally held to be superior to humanity. To this day, there are entire global communities that believe that directing their intentions to such "beings" allows them to negotiate a better outcome from the universe, improve their lot in life, or to avoid/mitigate some calamity.

Unfortunately, for those people, there is no one on the other end of the cosmic prayer line. Any effective outcome obtained by calling on an egregore is the result of their own ability to manipulate a plastic universe partially created through our interaction with it. Like a talented athlete thanking "god" when scoring in a sportsball event or a skilled salesman thanking "god" for all their wealth and success, they themselves are the actual engine that accomplished the goal, but they insist on giving credit to a non-existent entity.

In short, the worshipper of an egregore is just as capable of reaching a Trance or a state of Ekstasis during their attempts at supplication. The energy of that state is what results in their positive outcome, not the egregore.

However, the egregore serves a purpose in this case, because it allows the worshiper to perform much the same trick a magician does when encoding their intention into a sigil. The conscious responsibility of the worshiper is removed and transferred, by them, to the egregore. There is also the belief of those who worship the egregore which may have a positive impact on the desired outcome.

This is one of two ways that egregores can be effectively utilized: reaching a state of Ekstasis or Trance during a session of worship. The other way is to take advantage of all the energy and intentions directed towards an egregore by becoming the egregore yourself. Both are detailed in the two exercises below.

Part 2, Exercise 1: Exploiting Egregores through Worship

First, pick a mythology with active worshipers. In these days of globalism and multiculturalism, we have never been in a better position. From the monotheistic Abrahamic god(s) of the West to the polytheist pantheons of antiquity and the global South, the choices are nearly limitless. From pagan revivals of long dead spiritualities to the syncretism systems which grew out of the slave trade and Western imperialism, you can have your pick. Personally, I recommend selecting one of the polytheistic systems — these tend to have egregores in them which are more focused to a distinct area of responsibility. This can dovetail nicely into a specific intention. For this exercise, I've selected Hindu mythology.

Once you have your mythology, determine what you are trying to obtain via your worship. Select the egregore from that pantheon that most fits with what you are trying to accomplish. In this case, my objective is to get a promotion at work, so I'm going to select Ganesh, the remover of obstacles, to aid in getting the new position that I seek.

The next step is to go online or to a bookstore/library and research. This will give you ideas as to how to put together your ritual to obtain your objective. Pay attention to anything that specifically refers to the goal you have in mind—in my research, I found one site that noted uses of a standing, rather than a sitting, idol of Ganesh for "higher income"—great. So I go online and order one (at the time of this writing, they ranged from 20 U.S. dollars and up at most places I looked).

It doesn't have to be statuette; it can also be a picture or a poster of Ganesh (or whatever egregore you have chosen). Regardless, choose where you are going to place the item that represents the egregore. Some people turn a table, a low bookshelf, or even just a shelf into an "altar". Place the image or the idol of the egregore there. The "altar" is also where you will (optionally) burn incense and place offerings to the egregore. Not all egregores require either incense or offerings, but for those who do, another short bit of research will inform you of what fits. However, keep in mind that you can be creative and use whatever is at hand. For example, sometimes research will point to a specific type of say, flower, incense, or whatever, and it's just not obtainable—just find something similar which will substitute for it.

Next, figure out your ritual. The most effective method for working with egregores in this way when it comes to a ritual is to do the following:

1) Prepare a sigil beforehand that encapsulates your intention & select either a state of Ekstasis or Trance that you will use in step 5.
2) Light the incense you are using and/or place your offerings on the altar.
3) Recite, chant, or sing praise to the egregore in question. Usually going over their attributes and whatnot.
4) Ask for what you want, either directly or through

an encoded mantra statement. If you didn't put an offering on the altar at step 2, put it on now.

5) Charge your sigil via a state of Ekstasis or Trance.
6) Thank the egregore in advance for helping you.[58]
7) Walk away.

I will go over each of these steps in more detail below.

Step 1: My intention for the above was, "I will get a promotion at work," and for this example, I'm going to use Trance *specifically drumming with the sigil encoded via morse code). Much like with creating a mantra, I will remove the duplicate letters so the intention becomes: I W L G E T A P R O M N K - in morse code this comes out to: *** —*—** — —**—*—*— —**—*— — — — — —*—*— (note: I practice it repeatedly before starting to make sure I have the rhythm down. One can also rearrange the morse code letter order of the intention for smoother play).

Step 2: I light the incense and a candle that I have placed on the altar and pour a small cup of sake placed in front of the Ganesh idol as an offering.

Step 3: Recite prayer to Ganesh:

'Greetings and salutations to the supreme Lord Ganesha!
Breaker of Obstacles! Destroyer of barriers! Remover of all Impediments!
One tusk Ganesha! Single focused mind! Who shines like a million suns!
He who showers his blessings on us all, kindly remove anything in my way!'

---

[58] If this stage if anything is still burning / on fire or lit (like a candle) put it out. Safety first.

Step 4: Ask for what you want:[59] "GREP TONK MAWLI"

Step 5: Beat out the rhythm of the encoded intention until a deep Trance state occurs. During this process, one can also visualize Ganesh removing obstacles in your path. Once you reach that state, simply stop at a time that feels right to you.

Step 6: Thank the egregore:

'Lord Ganesha, he who breaks through all constraints, I
thank you for hearing my prayer!
Lord Ganesha, he who shatters all blockages, I thank you
for your blessing!
Lord Ganesha, he of the many plentitudes, I thank you
for accepting my offering!'

Step 7: Walk away.

That's it. Go on with your day/evening.

Part 2, Exercise 2 - Exploiting Egregores by becoming the Egregore

Exercise 1 above very much represents a classic approach to working with egregores within most systems. It is by far the type most commonly associated with religions the world over. However, it is certainly not the only way to work with an egregore. In some practices, it is not uncommon for one or more of an egregore's worshipers to become the egregore itself via possession during a ritual. Often referred to in those systems as "being ridden," the possession allows the worshipers to interact with the

---

[59] I've rearranged the letters of the intention from step 1 into a quick encoded statement.

egregore directly in the form of the person acting as the avatar of the being.

While this method has practical use within a group ritual, it can also be adapted by the individual practitioner to hijack the energy expended by others. The toxick magician thus may vampirize a congregation of worshipers in real time. Alternatively, they can even just assume that somewhere, someone(or a group of someones) is directing their intentions to the egregore that can be harvested in this manner. In the former case, time your ritual for when a known group is meeting and in the latter case, perform it whenever suits your schedule.

In either case the form of the ritual is much the same.

1)   Prepare a sigil beforehand that encapsulates your intention & select either a state of Ekstasis or Trance that you will use in step 3. Note: Extasis is the more commonly used in this exercise.[60]

2)   Have any offerings to the egregore on hand as you would have in Exercise 1 along with a method of destroying/consuming them in mind beforehand — burning, drinking, eating etc.[61]

3)   Assume the role of the egregore though a pre-selected method of Ekstasis or Trance.

4)   Once you have achieved possession, i.e. are the egregore, destroy your sigil. Any offerings are consumed or destroyed at this time as well.

5)   Exit the working area, and immediately engage in some mundane activity like washing the dishes, taking out

---

[60] It's also assumed that you've already got an egregore in mind and have done your research regarding it as was done for the first exercise.
[61] It's not uncommon in some systems to offer egregores consumables such as wine, hard alcohol, small cakes, fruit, etc. Or things that get burned or even killed like small animals or flowers or incense, etc. - I personally do not advocate animal sacrifice but it would be remiss to not mention that it is a thing.

the garbage/recycling, or watching a movie. The idea is to make a clean psychological break at the end of the working.

I will go over each of these steps in more detail below.

Step 1: For this example, we're going to stick with Ganesh as the egregore, but we're going to change things up a bit and switch from Trance (drumming) to Ekstasis (dance)[62]. The intention will remain the same: "I will get a promotion at work" — this will be changed into a pictographic sigil by first removing the duplicate letters leaving us (again) with: I W L G E T A P R O M. This can then be put together on a small piece of paper:

Step 2: Pour a cup of sake and light some incense.

Step 3: Dance into a state of Ekstasis. While doing so, envision yourself as Ganesh. You may assist this process by reciting some of the mantras associated with Ganesh while dancing. Keep focused on the pictographic sigil while doing so. As this goes on, envision all those praying to Ganesh as praying to you. See them making offerings to you, directing all their hopes and dreams to you. Examples

[62] For using Dance Ekstasis I recommend having pre-recorded quick tempo music playing. That is entirely optional but frankly, even alone, I would feel silly dancing without music. Start the music between step 2 and 3.

of Ganesha mantras:[63]

Om Gam Ganapataye Namaha - warding off negativity
Aum Gajānanāya Namah - for inner peace
Om Vighnanashaya Namah - removing obstacles

Step 4: At the height of Ekstasis, consume the sake, snuff out the incense, and destroy the sigil.

Step 5: Exit the working area and immediately engage in some mundane activity.

Part 3: Demons, daemons & Djin[64]

In addition to the egregores of mythology are lesser non-corporeal entities known as angels or demons, daemons, djinn, ghosts, spirits, etc. The list is practically endless, but all of them boil down to a non-god, non-corporeal agent which can be called upon to perform tasks or intercede with an egregore.

They are essentially premade agents. Use at your own risk. There exists at present dozens of works on goetic[65] magic with often extremely complex and convoluted methodologies for summoning entities of this type to execute the magician's will. If you find this type of byzantine exercise appealing, don't let me stop you from investigating the efficacy of goetic magic. My personal opinion is that you are better off making and breaking your own agents rather than plugging yourself into these legacy systems.

---

[63] Aayush - https://vedicfeed.com/powerful-ganesh-mantras/
[64] And I could add here fairies, angels, sprites, goblins, saints, etc. etc. etc.
[65] Goetic magic is the magic that deals with summoning demons.

Chapter 10
Transmogrification & Embracing the Anathema (eliminate limitations on self)

As others before me have pointed out, "the self", as it is classically known, isn't set in stone[66]. At least, it is not as set in stone as many would believe. Under the right circumstances, just about every aspect of what you think of as you is potentially changeable. What beliefs you hold can easily mutate due to stressful circumstances or can be imprinted on you during times of psychological vulnerability.

The same goes for other elements of the self: are you extroverted or introverted? A workaholic or perpetually lazy? Empathetic or callous? Kind or vicious? Punctual to a fault or consistently late? An early or a late riser? Fastidious or sloppy? Promiscuous or vanishingly shy? Progressive or conservative? ...etc. I should mention that the above listed traits and beliefs are not strictly either/or propositions. More often than not, we all fall along a spectrum, and few are extremely one thing or extremely another.

Additionally, as human beings, we routinely fall into patterns of behavior, habits, ways of thinking, of doing things, and of establishing routines. This results in predictability which can be an asset or a handicap depending on the circumstances.[67] Due to this, we can exploit the predictability of others to our advantage by relying on them to do as they have always done. Conversely, we can disrupt, disturb, thwart, or overturn the plans of others when it suits our purposes by breaking

---

[66] Peter Carroll makes this point in "Liber Null & Psychonaut" for example.

[67] It's been known to be downright fatal for those who already have a target on their back.

out of our own patterns and habits unexpectedly. This increases our potential range of future actions.

Having the ability to do this is a useful talent to possess, and it's one that can be learned through a combination of transmogrification and embracing what anathema is to us.

Transmogrification

Referring back to Section 1, Chapter 1 and journaling yourself, you should have a pretty good idea of how this process works. However, those exercises were more focused on establishing a baseline, setting goals, and reaching them. In the exercises below, your attention will be instead focused on metaphorically shaking things up. You will take what you do and think now and consciously alter them. Your habits, your experiences, and your beliefs are under your control (more than you might suspect), and you should practice changing them at will.

Exercise 1, Habit Modification

Make a list of your habits and come up with at least 5 to 10. For this exercise, take the following for example: the time you wake up, which hand is dominant, the route you take to work, what you typically eat, and the first thing you do when you get back home. This is just a sample list, and you should create one that is specific to you consisting of your personal habits. Obviously "the route you take to work" doesn't apply to you if you work from home or don't have a job, so substitute something that does apply, like "the route you take to school" or "the time you start working while home," etc.

Exercise 1, Habit 1 "The time you wake up"[68]

If you set an alarm each night to get up for work or school the next day, set it 5 minutes earlier tonight before going to bed, then 10 minutes the day after that, and so on. Continue until you are getting up an hour earlier than normal each day. On days when you are off and probably don't set an alarm, set one for time you usually get up on a day off, then 5 minutes earlier on the next day off and so forth. Don't bother to wake up more than 15 or 20 minutes earlier than usual on an off day unless you feel like extending the exercise to a full hour earlier as you are doing on workdays.

Obviously, this will extend the time between when you get up and when you normally leave for work giving you two options with this habit modification. Option 1 — identify an activity or hobby that you can fill time with, and then perform that activity or hobby during that time. Option 2 — if showing up early won't risk losing you your job, show up early. The first day, show up 5 minutes early, then 10, then 15, then 20. When you get to 25 or 30 minutes, feel free to start making the time you show up for work random, never show up late, but never show up at the same time. The extra time at work can be spent catching up on things or even just being social. Again, don't risk getting fired for this exercise. However, if you can get away with randomizing your arrival time at work, do so.

Exercise 1, Habit 2 "Which hand you use"

On the first day of this exercise, if you brush your teeth with your right hand, use your left, and vice versa. On the second day, continue to brush your teeth with your non-

---

[68] For some it might be more accurate to call this "the time you get out of bed"

dominant hand, and switch between whichever hand you usually use to comb and/or style your hair[69] with the one you usually don't. The third day, start opening doors with your non-dominant hand. Practice throwing a ball or dart with your non-dominant hand on the fourth day.[70] On the following day, start to eat and drink with your non-dominant hand. Continue to do all of the above concluding with taking 10 to 15 minutes to practice writing with the hand you don't normally write with (alternatively, if you spend a lot of time on an office computer with a mouse you can switch the mouse to the other hand).

The point of this exercise isn't to necessarily master ambidexterity, but instead to give you a foothold in that direction. Though, with enough time and effort, you should be able to switch back and forth at will.

Exercise 1, Habit 3 "The route you take to work"

Examine the route to take to go to work (or school), regardless of whether it is walking, biking, or driving. If possible, begin to take a different route every day. Switch from freeways to city streets or vice versa (again, if possible). Obviously don't risk being late, so give yourself extra time if you are doing this exercise. Do the same for trips to places you go regularly, such as grocery shopping, the gym, to a friend's house, or your favorite restaurant or bar. If you have the opportunity to vary your mode of transport (bike, car, bus, train, etc.), do so as well. The length of this exercise will vary depending on the number of trips you take and the number of locations you normally go to.

For locations that you do not have to reach at a set

---

[69] If you have it, obviously.
[70] If you don't own a ball, get one, they are cheap. Any ball will do but some are better if you're just throwing it around indoors. A tennis ball is a great example.

date/time, but which you normally do at a set date/time change, start showing up at a different time on the day you usually go. For example, if you shop on Saturdays for groceries at 2:00 PM, go at 1:45 the next time, then 2:15 the time after that, then 1:30, then 2:30, and so forth up to an hour (or two) earlier or later than normal. You could also change it to another day entirely depending on your availability.

At any point during this exercise you can switch back to what was your original habitual route before changing it up again. This exercise is open ended and can be stopped at any time or continued indefinitely.

Exercise 1, Habit 4 "Eating"

What and when we eat may feel like a matter of free choice, but in actuality, it is often determined by cultural expectations. Take a week and record what you typically eat and when you do so. Also, take the time to research various diets like intermittent fasting, vegetarianism, veganism, pescatarianism, keto, and so forth. Once you have done that, start to change what you eat. For example, you might eat breakfast food at what would be typically dinner time or lunch and vice versa, cooking what would normally be an evening meal in the morning, or, as with intermittent fasting, you might decide to not eat for a set amount of time — typically 16 hours of the day and only eat during the remaining 8[71]. Once you have experimented with eating different meals at the time it would typically be eaten for other meals, or have begun intermittent fasting, consider changing what types of food you consume — if you eat a lot of meat, consider switching to

---

[71] And yes, some of those 16 hours should be during the time you normally sleep. Ideally, stop eating 4 hours before you go to bed, and don't eat until after being awake for 4 hours (presuming you typically sleep 8).

vegetarianism. If you are a vegetarian, consider switching to pescatarianism [72], or slowly adding meat to your meals (chicken is a good place to start). If you are a vegetarian, consider switching to veganism for a while, or vice versa if you are a vegan. Between a spectrum of veganism on the one extreme and an entirely carnivore diet on the other extreme, there are a whole range of possible dietary rules you can set (and break) for yourself. Consider eating a diet type for a set period of time, like a week or a month, and then settle on one that works best for you.

The ultimate purpose of this part of the exercise isn't to find the best diet for you, though it can be used to do so–the ultimate purpose of this part of the working is to break out the dietary pattern and lifestyle you have become accustomed to.

Exercise 1, Habit 5 "What you do when you get home"

Some people might be at a loss if asked, "What do you typically do when you get home?" or "what do you do in your free time?" Take a week to note down what you do during the time between when you get home from work or school (or if you work from home, what you do when you are finally off the clock) and when you go to bed. Some have very structured free time, others not so much. Even those with no free time agenda often follow a pattern. Perhaps they always stop at the corner bar for a drink before getting home or always have one right when they walk in the door. Maybe they always turn on the TV or ask their partner how their day was. From there, it's usual for people to go through the same routine day after day, night after night, with little or no variation. This part of the exercise is to shake that up.

After you have noted what you normally do each and

---

[72] A vegetarian that also eats seafood (i.e. fish, shrimp, etc)

every evening in a typical week, start to add, remove, and change what and when you do it. You can start by modifying something simple like the time you go to bed: go to bed 15 minutes early or later, then 30 minutes, then 45, etc. If you stay in most nights, consider going out instead (if you have the means). This can be as simple as just going for a walk or to pick up something trivial from the local shop. If you typically have an alcoholic drink when you get home, have something else or refrain entirely for a few days. Come up with a to do list before you get home and execute it. Take care of things that you would normally have done on your day off instead. The ultimate goal is to be able to, at will, change any and every element of what would normally constitute your typical evening.

When you have broken out of your evening/after work patterns you can return to your original evening habits, or you can continue changing them randomly. Like the modification of the route to take to work, this exercise can be concluded when you feel that you've broken out of your old habits or you can continue this exercise indefinitely.

Exercise 2, Experience Modification

How we experience the world, the things we choose to watch, read, listen to, and do ultimately impact how we fit into the world. For some, it's often the defining element of "who they are"; their taste or obsession in a type of musical subculture, for example, can evolve into an entire personality for them. The same can be said for certain hobbies, pastimes, and activities. Those involved in them can often be defined by them. They fit neatly into the box defined by their subculture. If you find yourself thus situated, it is time to break out of it. If you don't find yourself narrowly defined in this way, it's time to experiment with it.

For this exercise select three subcultures, the only caveat being that you do not currently belong to one of them. Research each in turn, and then become involved in each sequentially over a set period of time. You can do all three within a year (four months for each), or even extend this exercise out to three years, changing which subculture you are in annually. You don't have to limit yourself to three; you can continue doing this exercise indefinitely, or you can stop it at any time. The experience of more than one subculture is what matters. Moreover, it is not enough to simply say you are part of "x" subculture. Once you get into it you must reach out to those already involved and establish a social network within the subculture. This will be important for later exercises in Section 3 of this book.

Feel free to select any subculture. In no particular order, I have listed a small sample below. Feel free to look around, though. Don't consider yourself limited to the ones I have listed.

Punk
Goth
· Steampunk
Straight-edge
Gamers
Ravers
Cyberpunk
Hipsters
Bronies
Bikers
Vsco Girls
Egirls & Eboys

Exercise 3, Belief Modification

If you weren't raised by wolves, you grew up in a specific cultural milieu by a parent or parents/guardians that taught you a set of beliefs. These were in turn imparted on them by their parents, and so on and so forth, generation upon generation. Naturally, there may have been breaks. Sometimes an ancestor experienced a religious or political conversion, emigrated to another country, etc., which altered how they subsequently raised their own offspring, but, by and large, beliefs pass mostly unchanged and unchallenged from one generation to the next.

Naturally, many rebel a bit during their teenage years, and then, as they age, fall back into their parents beliefs, but a few do make a clean break. I remember one acquaintance who was raised a conservative catholic, got into alternative spiritualities, became a pagan, subsequently got into chaos magic, left chaos magic to go back to paganism, and finally, wound up right back where they started as a catholic. Frankly, apart from the experience gained, it was a complete waste of time.

Never go back to where you started. Keep moving forward and experience new things perpetually. The best way to do so is by regularly shaking up your beliefs. Exercise 2 above should assist you in getting started with this exercise. In moving from one subculture to the next, you were exposed to the beliefs and preconceptions of the people involved in those social groups. In this exercise, you will continue to move forward by consciously changing your politics and practice moving into new paradigms. Along with Exercise 2, this exercise is crucial for work done in Section 3.

Exercise 3, Belief 1 "Politics"

From anarchists to fascists, paleo-conservatives to neo-liberals, and everything in between, hanging off at every conceivable angle, there are a myriad of political parties and groups in our world today. Depending on where you live, there might be only two viable political parties that hold power, or three, or four or dozens. Regardless, these are where you should focus your attention.

First, identify the viable political groups in your country. Pick one. Research that group, its beliefs, and positions, the arguments that they use to defend them, the people who are involved in the party, etc. Next, become actively involved. Yes, this will involve work. Online activism is a good start, to be sure, but actual, viable, political parties have local chapters, grassroots organizers, elected officials, and candidates for office, etc. Volunteer and get involved with them.

While the time invested by you is entirely up to you, I recommend staying involved through and beyond at least one election cycle. For example, in my country, we have elections quite frequently, but most are every two years with some being every four. Stay involved during that entire time, and most importantly, network. Grow your contact list within the party as much as you can. If possible, maintain contact even when you take the next step.

The next step is to switch parties.[73] You read that right. Switch parties. Pick one of the others you identified from above and go through this exercise again. This time, you will participate on the other side of the proverbial political fence. Note, this has the potential to be incredibly disruptive. It may involve losing friends and ending relationships. If that is a risk you don't want to take, or an impact that you feel would have too much of a detrimental impact on your economic or family situation you should feel free to not go forward with this. Alternatively, many political parties in countries that have, say, just two, have factions within the party itself — if that is the case, switch factions.

---

[73] Of course, should you somehow find yourself living in a one-party state, switching parties isn't possible. If you do find yourself in a one-party state, I recommend getting the fuck out of there. If that is impossible, there are often factions within the party. So instead of parties, switch factions.

Joshua Wetzel

Regardless of whether you switch factions or switch parties, continue with the rest of the steps described in paragraph two of this section. I also recommend being involved for at least the same amount of time, as mentioned above in paragraph three.

Exercise 3, Belief 2 "Paradigms"

This exercise will involve the process of shifting between one set of spiritual or religious beliefs and then another (and another and another). As with political groups, there may only be a few in your location which are of any significance. These should be your primary focus. As with politics, first identify them, if you don't know them all already. Pick one, then research that group, its beliefs and positions, and the arguments that they used to defend them. Read any relevant texts or books regarding the one you select. Finally, become actively involved. As with a political belief, you can start online, but the real value is in interacting with actual people in your area. If there are none in your area, it is acceptable to conduct this exercise wholly on the internet.

The time you stay involved with the group is entirely up to you, but I recommend a time frame of no less than one year with the ideal amount of time being between two and five years. During that time, be actively involved. Go to meetings, services, or whatever gatherings that they have. Grow your list of contacts within the group as much as you reasonably can. Be a visible member of their community as much as possible. In other words, be involved.

After a period of time, paradigm shift. Leave the group and join another one identified as in the first step above. As with politics, this does have the potential for some disruption in your life. Depending on your situation, you may wish to take advantage of the fact that many religions have sects within them, much like factions within political parties. It is often possible to change sects and not burn all your bridges with your current associates. Regardless of whether you shift paradigms entirely or migrate between sects within a paradigm, continue as you did before. Rinse and repeat.

I'd like to mention some cautionary notes here. Be very thorough in your research. Some groups are very easy to join and very hard to leave. Some religions, for example, outright call for the murder of those who leave them. Others stop short of this, but instead attempt to destroy the lives of those who leave. I would, if at all possible, steer clear of these religions and groups. The objective of this exercise is to break through the chains of belief, not to put ourselves at the risk of actual harm. I would also stay clear of any group that requires a large financial obligation. If they do, odds are they only want your money, and being one of them doesn't add any real value to your life.

A final recommendation for which spiritual or religious groups you consider joining—pick those that have a magical or shamanic element to them. This may allow any magick that you do to fly under the radar, as the group already has practices along those lines. So, to recap the recommendations: the group should be relatively easy to join and to leave, it should not be a massive financial drain, and some magical, shamanic, or magick-like practices should be a part of it in some fashion.

Exercise 4, Embracing the Anathema

The last restriction anyone has is toward the things that they find disgusting, abhorrent, or whatever term you choose to mean; "this is the list of things I will NOT do, period, end of story." That is anathema to you. It certainly varies wildly from person to person. One individual's anathema can be another person's kink. Some people also have phobias, which I believe fall under this definition of "nope". Coming up with a list of things that you will not do is, in short, harder for some people than for others. However, regardless of where you start with this exercise, there is probably still a list of things that you have not or will not do.

The first step is to identify things that you have refused to do for whatever reason. These reasons can be cultural, religious, social, sexual, or personal. As indicated above, this list can be long or short depending on your worldly experience. Yet, even with that, odds are there are still items that remain. List these activities or actions. These will be what you use to accomplish this exercise.

The next step is to remove any things from that list that would have severe negative health outcomes. If doing it would put your life at risk, don't do it. Most people wouldn't, for example, eat their own (or anyone else's) excrement. There is a good reason for this—if you eat your own shit, it can kill you. So don't. Nor should you jump out of a 10-storey window. That's not embracing the anathema, that's committing suicide. Don't do it.

That being said, most people would also avoid drinking their own piss, but doing so won't kill you. Nor would going to an extremely high place when you have a fear of heights.[74] Eating insects won't kill you either (depending on the insect, research is always key before doing anything), nor would engaging in a sexual practice that you currently do not.[75] While I cannot give you a list of examples, because it would be impossible to cover the anathemas of all the people out there, I can state that they fall into the categories hinted at above.

---

[74] Yes, failing from such a place could be fatal, but if you take precautions, and high places are what you avoid, it's a good example.
[75] Regardless, practice safe sex. I know I shouldn't have to add this here, but I feel that I must. Don't do anything that will risk imminent death or disease. That would be counterproductive to this exercise.

1) Things that are ingested.
2) Activities which activate phobias.
3) Deviations from sexual norms.

So, if you are an arachnophobe, you may wish to get a pet spider. If you are afraid of heights, you may wish to take up rock climbing. If you are a strict vegan, you may wish to start eating meat, or if you are a meat eater, you may wish to go full vegan. If you have no sexual kink, you may wish to experiment with one or experiment with your own sexuality. Much depends on the individual's own limitations.

The final step is to research how to do what you are planning on doing so as to not risk death or permanent injury to yourself. This is key. The point of this exercise is to increase the likelihood that you will do anything at any point when that thing needs doing. Not only that, you will do it in such a way that you come out unscathed. So, research is extremely important.

Also, don't do anything that will get you arrested. Most of us are not criminals, and while you could, for example, steal something if you find the idea of theft anathema, I would not recommend it. The same goes for any crime. "Jail" rhymes with "fail" for a reason, in my opinion. If you find yourself there, you've most definitely failed. Maybe not permanently, but certainly at the time.

Through the process of transmogrification and embracing the anathema, the practitioner of toxick magick breaks the limitations that are placed on the self. The magician becomes flexible, capable of changing habits and beliefs at will. This will allow one to more easily reach goals and obtain results. Rather than controlling you, you now control these facets of yourself.

Chapter 11
Strategic Magick

When it comes to using magick, there is more to consider than just "I want x," then firing off a sigil to get what you desire. There are two other legs to the stool when it comes to "getting what you want." The first leg is identifying and removing obstacles strategically. The other is creating avenues of manifestation, which we go over in the next chapter. Combined with the use of a state of Trance or Ekstasis in a reality engineering event, success will be achieved if you use these three things in concert.

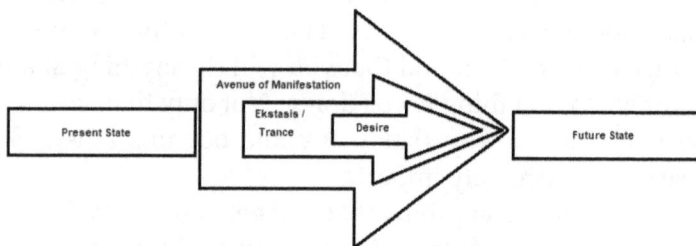

Avenue of Manifestation

Present State — Ekstasis / Trance — Desire → Future State

Traditionally, the identification and removal of obstacles in magick broadly fell under the umbrella of "red" or "war" magick. This, however, is a very limited way of looking at using this type of magick. Just using "war" magick to "Hulk Smash!" lacks any kind of strategic thinking. Your only tool isn't a metaphorical hammer, and thus all your problems are not (nor will they ever be) just metaphorical nails.[76]

Often, the best way to overcome a confrontational

---

[76] I'm not saying that someone isn't going to, at some point, piss you off so much that you want to burn their life to the fucking ground. I'm just saying that that scenario is one of many confrontational ones that you may encounter.

situation (magical or mundane) isn't a direct attack. In fact, regarding the mundane, I would go farther and say, "If you find yourself in a fist fight...you've already lost, regardless of the outcome." In terms of magical situations, if your only resource is cursing someone to death, you've already lost whatever confrontation has or might occur.

That being said, strategic magick involves a number of other ways of handling adversarial or competitive situations. These consist of inflationary attacks, win-win attacks, substitution attacks, indirect attacks, and finally, when there is no other option left, direct attacks.[77] Additionally, these can be mixed and matched for optimal outcomes. I'll go over each type of attack in turn and provide examples below. I will also give examples of using some of them together to fully round out the lesson.

Inflationary Attack

When faced with opposition to reaching your goal, such as situations where someone is already in possession of it or they are deliberately trying to keep you from obtaining it out of malice, one of the best tactical approaches is the inflationary attack. The inflationary strategy involves not cursing the opposition per se, but instead relies on directing positive Ekstasis or Trance energy towards the target. The idea being to take advantage of whatever bad habits or tendencies they have in order to cause them to self-destruct. Thus, removing them from the picture and allowing you to, hopefully, obtain your goal.

You can use either sigils or agents to help focus energy towards the target using your preferred method of Trance

---

[77] "To fight and conquer in all your battles is not supreme excellence; supreme excellence consists in breaking the enemy's resistance without fighting." - Sun Tzu, The Art of War

or Ekstasis to charge the intention. That being said, the best combination I've found is a sigil used with Trance. The sigil is a simple encoded statement along the lines of, "It is my will to direct positive energy to <target>." Enter Trance via your preferred method while focusing on an image of your opponent in your mind's eye.

This strategy can easily be used in conjunction with creating a mundane avenue of manifestation. If you are personally close to the target, you might already have an idea of what their particular Achilles' heel is. If they are prone to bouts of rage, you might feed them information or steer them into stressful situations where flying off the handle is more likely. If they have an addictive personality, you might facilitate their access to their drug of choice. If they are hiding something, but happen to be of a loquacious nature, you might work towards having them blurt it out.

The only cautionary note I would sound here is that this might backfire if your target realizes that you are manipulating them or their environment. So, make sure to cover your tracks. How? You might work through a 3rd party who is either willing to help you or who would unwittingly carry out your intention, all the while believing that they were doing something good for the target. You might also get to them anonymously, something which the internet and even the old-fashioned mail can facilitate.

If properly executed, the target will self-destruct without the messiness of a direct confrontation, thus allowing the opening you need to reach your objective. This strategy has the added bonus of the target being left with no other conclusion but to blame themselves. After all, it was their own wants, desires, bad habits, or tendencies that caused them to lose their grip on what you were after. They can't blame you for obtaining it, you just happened to be around to step in when they fell apart.

Win-Win Attack

There is a well-known parable about two sisters fighting over an orange. They both want it for their own purpose and are reluctant to have their other sister take all of it. Finally, after much back and forth, they agree to split the orange in half, each settling for less than what they had hoped for but at least getting something. However, it turns out that one needed the rind, while the other needed the pulp. Had this been properly communicated, each would have gotten what they had wanted, which would have resulted in a "win-win" situation.

The win-win strategy involves helping your opponent reach an objective which also benefits you in the process. The magick is the same as if you yourself were trying to obtain a particular goal, but instead you work to make the goal of your competition a reality for them. The sigil phrasing is simple: "It is my will that <x> obtain their goal" and you can use any form of Ekstasis or Trance to charge the intention.

In terms of creating a mundane avenue of manifestation, you can work towards helping them reach their goal if that is within your means. Much like with the inflationary strategy, you help them to get what they are after knowing that, in the end, it will benefit you as much or more. The difference between going the win-win route vs the inflationary attack is that you **don't** want to be anonymous unless the situation calls for anonymity. Visibility is key so that the target will desire to reciprocate and will want to help you obtain your goal.

The clear advantage in using this approach is that everyone comes out ahead. You help them get what they want, and they, in turn, help you to get what you want. There really is no down-side to this approach. While the world may be finite, that doesn't mean that we have to play zero-sum games where one person wins and the other loses. In the right circumstances, and with the right strategies, everyone involved can come out a winner.

Substitution Attack

This strategy is related to the win-win approach but is more concerned with you getting what you want regardless of whether or not the target also obtains their objective. The way this is done is by multiplying the choices available to your opponent. If they have, or are trying to obtain, a resource that you also wish to acquire, you work to manifest additional versions or instances of that objective. For example — if you were, say, competing for a job role, you might phrase your intention as, "It is my will that <target> will get other job offers," or a variation of that, charged with whatever form of Trance or Ekstasis works best for you.

Ideally, your adversary will become like the mule starving to death between two (or more) bales of hay. Too many choices can have a paralyzing effect. The goal is to put them in that situation. As with the win-win strategy, you can also actively be the one that places these choices in front of them, if the circumstances allow you to do so. Obviously, it doesn't even have to be you if you can work through a proxy. Either way, the target is distracted by options, and the way to your objective is opened for you.

Indirect Attack

Sometimes the best way to destroy someone is to not go after them directly but go after the things and people that they care about. Just about everyone has a circle of friends and acquaintances, coworkers and family, career and possessions. Targeting these people and things can often destabilize and destroy an enemy far more effectively than going after them point-blank. In this scenario, the goal is to obtain your objective by plunging your opponent's world into chaos. If their life is burning down around them (either figuratively or literally), they won't have the time or energy to get in your way.

The first step in this process is reconnaissance. As Sun Tzu wrote in *The Art of War*, "To know your enemy and know yourself is to not fear the outcome of a hundred confrontations." So, find out all there is to know about your adversary through whatever means are available to you. Thanks to our online social lives these days, this is often ridiculously easy. People will often post and tweet just about everything there is to know about themselves. Take advantage of that, if you can, to gather information about the target.

In addition to observing your foe online (or even if you can't gain access to their online activity), consider some good old fashioned mundane spying. If you know them personally, you can even be your own spy. People, as a rule, love talking about themselves. Make sure to ask leading questions, and then listen carefully to the responses you get. When they reveal what interests them, cultivate the appearance of being interested in it yourself. Ultimately, the goal here is to get them to talk about their lives so as to uncover where to hit them where it hurts the most. If you don't have personal access to your target, identify and befriend subjects close to them. Once befriended, you can use these individuals to gain information on the target or even get close to your enemy yourself through their friend (or friends). Either way, get to know them as well as you know yourself.

The second step is to sift through the information you have obtained and determine who or what is most important to your rival. This will often be their Achilles' heel. It is this person, place or thing that will be your actual target. Their career, family, and cherished possessions are often high on this list. You should direct any magical attack towards these people or things, thus crippling your enemy without striking them directly. If they are unaware that you are their enemy, you can even be there for emotional support as your actions take effect — adding a dash of schadenfreude to the mix.

If you have the ability to sabotage their career or damage their beloved possessions in a mundane way, you should consider doing this, but also remember that if you break local laws in the process, it's on you if you get caught and punished. With the strategy of indirect attack, I recommend avoiding any action which could be directly traced back to you. For example, if you become aware, say, that the target is engaged in illegal activity at work and you have the opportunity to report them anonymously, then do so. The same goes for the people close to them: if you uncover a way to cause them distress in the above fashion, do it.

On the other hand, if your adversary really loves their car, think twice before slashing its tires, keying it, or pouring sugar in the gas tank — if someone catches you in the act, it would have been better for you to have done nothing. The same goes for any action against an actual person. I advise against any illegal moves. Curse their family with magick if family is what is most important to them, but don't lash out in the mundane world, for the simple reason that if you get caught (and more get caught than don't), you will go to jail, and going to jail = losing.

Direct Attack

If no other options are available to you, then cursing your enemy directly is the last strategy on the table. Peter Carroll mentions in *Liber Null & Psychonaut* a tactic known as "the death fast" — where you, the practitioner, refrain from food for an extended period of time, all the while focusing the suffering and pain you experience not eating at your nemesis.[78] This is a valid method of cursing, to be sure. Alternatively, if you have an image of your target (or even just their name) sigilized on a piece of paper, you can work yourself into a state of rage Ekstasis while focusing on that sigil. This method doesn't even require a specific intention—it's just directing hateful energy their way. If you have progressed well in your physical, emotional, and mental control up to this point and have a good working knowledge of Ekstasis and Trance, you will be capable of inflicting a great deal of misfortune this way.

Ultimately, the goal of Carroll's death fast is in the name—the death of your opponent—however, I personally find that result distinctly unsatisfying. Death is the end of suffering, and if you truly hate someone you should want to increase their misery and prolong their suffering as much as possible. Any written intention should definitely be along these lines, should you choose to be more specific, than just directing hate Ekstasis.

In conclusion, the way to get what you want is best achieved by the use of strategy. Combine that with the solid execution of a reality engineering event, utilizing a state of Trance or Ekstasis. Lastly, throw in the mundane methods of opening avenues of manifestation (which we will cover in the next chapter), and you will reach your objectives.

---

[78] As with any fasting, I recommend staying hydrated. Water is not food, so it doesn't break the fast.

Chapter 12
Creating Avenues of Manifestation

One of the most routine, rookie mistakes any practitioner of magick can make is that of performing an act of results oriented magick while simultaneously ignoring any possible environmental constraints that might stand in their way. Put another way, the magician executes their ritual, and then sits back and waits for the result, without putting forth any mundane effort to help it come to pass. In short, they fail to create an avenue of manifestation for the desired effect to manifest. This is a recipe for failure. While there are some results that can be expected to occur without any engagement on your part of the ritual itself, there are others that stand no chance of becoming reality, unless you yourself provide an open avenue for the energy and intent you are releasing into the universe.

In using magick, it's a common mistake to think of the act of extending your will as being sufficient. This is not the case. Thinking like that is akin to someone in a game of bowling believing that, to wish hard enough, a strike will occur, and that once the wish is made, the ball will miraculously hurl itself down the lane towards the pins and knock them all down. More realistically, seeking your results without magick is akin to a casual bowler just aiming and rolling the ball, hoping for the best. Using magick is like having the skills not only to aim the ball, but to put the optimal spin on it to achieve a strike.

Examples of failure along these lines are too many to count. I myself have been guilty of this mistake, and I dare say the vast majority of occultists have had the same experience. However, there is one story which sticks in my mind. Years ago, I met another magician who was in some distress, because he had performed what he felt had been, at the time, a solid ritual. He had done everything to the best of his ability, but the outcome was a disaster, and he asked me if I had any suggestions. Seeking to understand what went wrong, I began asking some questions. "What was the objective?" He replied, "To pass an exam." I followed up with, "Did you study?" at which point, a rather stunned expression crossed his face.

It would be common sense to anyone else that studying for a test was the only way to pass one. To my friend, that conclusion ran against the grain of the notion expressed in chaos magick: that if you execute a ritual 100% correctly, with perfect Gnosis (read Trance or Ekstasis), have a perfect magical link to the target, completely destroy any subconscious resistance, and have no "lust of result," you will succeed 100% of the time[79]. One could even go so far as to say that divorcing your magick from your reality in such a way is a fundamental flaw at the heart of the chaos magick system.

There is only one case I can think of where being diligent in terms of laying down a solid mundane avenue of manifestation can be skipped. That would be for objectives that already have a high probability of occurring on their own. Like, if you hated a trapeze artist who was notoriously slipshod when it came to their safety, and you cursed them to have an accident. The same would go for any situation that breaks down to having and executing an intent that's already bound to happen; reality is already doing the work for you. You don't have to risk getting caught replacing one of their ropes with a worn out one. They are already using ropes and lines that aren't properly maintained.[80]

Beyond the above example, any magick should have a

---

[79] This if of course laying aside the fact that doing any complex activity 100% correctly, without a mistake of any kind is a rather unrealistic expectation to hold.

[80] This example is entirely fictional and is no way factual in any way, shape or form.

mundane assist. You can do magick all the livelong day in order to have people you despise come to grief, attract new sexual partners, or get a great job. However, if you don't discover an opponent's weaknesses and exploit them, don't clean yourself up, acquire a skill that others value, get some exercise, stop eating crap, or don't have what an employer is looking for, nothing will happen.

Let us look at two of the above objectives but we'll skip the first objective: people you despise coming to grief as it is covered in the proceeding chapter. So, starting with attracting a new sexual partner. What are the mundane avenues of manifestation that apply? Well, they fall under a couple of categories. First—personal appearance and hygiene—you have to not look like shit, and you better not stink of either filth or desperation. People can smell desperation, and it's the ultimate anti-aphrodisiac. Secondly, there has to be something about you that another person wants. Acquire that. Where you are in this regard determines how far you have to go in order to lay the proper groundwork.

Do you already take good care of yourself? If not, start. Do you already exercise on a regular basis? If not, start. What is it that a potential partner might find interesting? Whatever that is, do that. In other words, get really, REALLY good at something if you can. Yes, this takes time. Set aside that time. Know that you might not get said partner for a year (or even a bit more). Focus on health, appearance, and a hobby/enterprise/talent/activity.

Focus is the key here. Do NOT focus on pursuing a relationship. Focus on self, self-improvement, and self-aggrandizement. Focus on YOU. Often this will be enough. In the pursuit of a hobby or skill, you might run into someone else by chance who also is engaged in said activity, and success will happen. Great. If not, move onto the next avenue of manifestation.

Put yourself out there and network. You are well

groomed, you take care of yourself, and you're getting into better shape all the time; you have a talent, an area of expertise, or a skill, both of which were acquired through avenues one and two. Yet, the cliche still holds: 90% of winning is showing up. So, network with people who share your interests. Odds are, one of them will be appealing to you and vice versa. Another option is to simply get on a dating app and go. People today have far better options than a few decades ago when "putting yourself out there" meant going to a club and hoping you happened to run into someone that found you attractive.

Now, let's look at another objective: getting a great job (career) and the mundane avenues of manifestation that can facilitate making it a reality for you. Appearance and hygiene matter for this objective as well. Though some folks might doubt this assertion when it comes to the coworkers currently around them, it is generally necessary. In a broader sense, what is needed is a desirable skill set and the ability to sell a product. Though in this case, the product is you. The key element is to find something that, even if it doesn't thrill you, you can at least tolerate doing day in and day out.

In terms of a desirable skill set, acquire one. Naturally, this is harder than it sounds. Some people have the luxury of attempting many career paths or, if still in school, pursuing many different majors before settling on the one that works for them. Others have needs which are more immediate — food, shelter, bills that have to get paid, etc. If that's the case, take the shit job for now, but burn your evenings/off-time pursuing other possibilities. Yes, this will mostly preclude anything which could be called a social life, but that's the sacrifice that needs to be made.

Note, I said "mostly preclude." If you have a circle of friends with decent careers, or who are relatively connected, they just might present you with an opportunity that you might otherwise have missed.

Finding a lucrative career may start with something as simple as a question to your friends; "Is anyone into (x) or know someone who is?" Family can play a role here too. Never shy away from nepotism if it can be used to your advantage, even if that "advantage" is just getting a shit job to get you by while you go after a more lucrative one.[81]

The final element of this is a psychological trick played by yourself, on yourself, and on everyone around you. Convince yourself that you are a "hard worker" and that you get what you have achieved by dint of your "hard work". Take this attitude and apply it to every endeavor. Through it you can build up a mini cult of personality. Done correctly and initially validated by your actions, it will stick in people's minds so firmly that you may even find yourself in a position where you get paid far more than what you are worth, working far less than you would otherwise need to. Once established, an impression like that is hard to destroy.

Creating avenues of manifestation takes time and effort but it also ensures reward. And I know, a lot of people get into doing magick as an excuse to NOT have to slog through life towards objectives like everyone else. Just wave the proverbial magick wand and "Presto!" result. The sad fact is, you still have to slog, but with a magical assist you're pulling a cart and not dragging a sledge. You have an edge. Take advantage of it. But don't think it alone will solve every situation.

---

[81] A word about shit jobs, even when you leave them eventually - do NOT burn those bridges. The interconnected world today is a mixed blessing but one positive element of it is the ability to fall back on your network of associates, family and friends when push comes to shove.

Chapter 13
Purpose (magick without bullshit)

One of the saddest moments of my life was back in about 2006. I had to bail my alcoholic father out of jail after his 3rd or 4th OWI arrest. I was clearly tired, but in a good mood, as I dropped him off at the motel where he lived. At that moment he (still drunk mind you, even after about 7 or 8 hours in jail) made a snide comment about how it "must be nice to have a purpose in life" directed at me. I didn't respond with what needed to be said. I replied with, "Father, if you haven't figured out at your age that you, and only you, are responsible for giving yourself a purpose in life, you never will." I just shook my head and left. I haven't seen him since.

He was clearly miserable. To him, the universe was a chaotic, random, purposeless, and mindless place. Anyone who claimed to have a purpose in life was just fooling themselves, since it was ultimately meaningless. There was no god, afterlife, etc. So, why bother to do anything? It's a sad and ultimately fair question, but it has an answer that doesn't have to be rooted in religious or spiritual beliefs of any kind.[82] You give yourself a purpose in life, end of story.

Is giving yourself a purpose in life ultimately an arbitrary act without any inherent meaning? For myself, the answer is only slightly yes, but mostly no. Yes, in the sense of spinning galaxies. Your life, my life, even the lives of the most successful, richest, and most famous people — meaningless. However, change the scope. Shrink it down to you, your friends, lovers, family, coworkers, neighbors, and even fellow citizens. Suddenly, what you do *has* an impact. To yourself, to them, and even to people you might never meet.

---

[82] Though for billions, yeah, that's the way they go...but billions of people on our planet are also morons... so there's that.

Therefore, it behooves you to create a purpose for yourself: a goal, a pursuit, a hobby, an area of interest that you study. Beyond pursuing your purpose in life, many people do this crazy thing called "having shared interests." This immediately creates a social environment where your own words and actions will have an impact. This social environment is the venue in which to apply the techniques and principles found in this book.

Having a self-defined purpose is just the start. Be aware that you might have to do some mental housekeeping. That is to say, work that involves throwing out attitudes and beliefs which may be more of a handicap than a help. Many who get into magick are hamstrung by a set of beliefs that serve no other purpose than to keep them from getting what they want. These must be identified and removed. Finally, one should avoid certain modes of thinking that are ultimately counterproductive or detrimental to your happiness and success. I'll go over these below.

The Illusion of Cosmic Balance & False Restraints

A number of spiritual and magical systems have baked into them a belief in the notion of cosmic balance. This is the mistaken idea that for every bad thing done there must be some form of punishment meted out by the universe. Conversely, there must be some form of reward for every good action, as if the cosmos was simultaneously a traffic cop and magick Pez dispenser. Naturally, this way of thinking springs out of a very natural human desire for justice. As a rule, it's perfectly normal to want to punish someone doing harm and reward someone doing good. In the societies we have constructed, we have even gone so far as to create arbitrary rules (read laws) which serve this function. Remember that those rules are human constructs.

They have no underlying foundation in the natural world. A criminal who breaks one of those rules isn't punished by the universe. They are only punished by their fellow citizens and only IF they get caught in the act or are found out afterwards.

The fact that reality gives zero shits did not go unnoticed by those who, in the past, held temporal or spiritual authority in their communities. Aware that it was impossible to police the actions of everyone, everywhere, at all times, they concocted a plethora of systems designed to result in individuals policing themselves. Children were indoctrinated (read brain-washed) into thinking that if mommy or daddy didn't punish them for their transgressions, then the universe would make them suffer in some fashion in this life, the afterlife, or the next life. Adults raised in this fashion then readily impose this way of thinking on the next generation, and so on and so forth.

For the authorities in a society, this lie and the subsequent self-policing it creates, is an incredible boon, as it helps maintain the status quo. This status quo assists those in positions of power, wealth, and authority with everyone else being kept in their proper place, powerless, and exploited. Those who act out not only fear getting caught and punished by mundane authorities should they do something illegal, but they also tremble at the thought of spiritual repercussions.

The toxick magician should break free from these false restraints, regardless of what form they come in, and they come in many. From the notions of samsara and karma invented by South Asian religions[83] to the heaven and hell created by the Abrahamic faiths[84], to the joke which is the neo-pagan "threefold law" and mistaken notions of

---

[83] Hinduism, Jainism, Buddhism, etc.
[84] Judaism, Christianity and Islam (though to be fair, much less so in the Jewish faith than the other two).

destiny, fate, or predestination, all of them should be thrown into the metaphorical trash bin. Each one functions as a means of social control. Control imposed on you by someone else is never for your benefit, and the most insidious form of this hostile control is that which you impose on yourself in the name of someone or something else. Should you find yourself mired in any of these beliefs, cast them off and refrain from ever donning the chains forged by someone else's need to control you.

Mental Dead Ends

Redefining failure as success: if you find yourself living as an unemployed meth addict turning tricks to score drugs, you're not an anti-establishment rebel/entrepreneur sticking it to "the man" by not joining the corporate rat race — you are, in fact, a loser. The fact of the matter is, there is no shame in this. Everyone fails from time to time, sometimes in small ways, sometimes in truly epic fashion. The solution to failure isn't to pretend that it's another kind of success; it isn't.

The solution is to analyze the mistakes and missteps you have made and figure out the following: Can I correct the mistake? If I can't correct it, what can I learn from my mistake/mistakes in order to not repeat it/them? What steps can I take to dig myself out of the hole I've made for myself? Often, we know the solution to our problems but lack the will to undertake it. If the answers to your problems seem too daunting a challenge, ask yourself, "Can I break this solution down into smaller, more manageable steps?" Much like the recovering alcoholic taking it one day at a time, long-term success is often built one tiny step at a time.

Beware of anyone who goes around in public forums claiming that they are going to "own their power," especially if they run with this line after a personal disaster. If someone is looking for others to validate how they "own their power" by patting themselves on the head and telling others how wonderful they are, they have no power. The truly powerful are secure and have no need to seek such validation. Spend less time proclaiming that you are going to "own your power" and more time actually fixing your shit.

Which actually brings me to the next mental dead end — self-esteem: the idea that you have inherent value just because you are you and therefore don't have to strive to be of use to anyone else is a trap. It's a trap used by those who are in positions of power and authority to keep you satisfied with where you find yourself now; don't fall for it. The doctrine of self-esteem is a type of social control. Like the carrots and sticks comprising the false restraints listed above, you, too, can preach self-esteem to people you want to hold back, but don't let others foist it on you. Until you have reached some point in your life where you are needed, valued, and desired, you are not entitled to self-esteem.

This isn't to say you can't feel good about being you, but there is feeling good because you are working towards your goals on the one hand, and there is unwarranted self satisfaction on the other. The former reinforces one's desire to go on, the latter drains the will and stymies forward progress. You don't have to be a joyless goat to obtain success in life, but you also shouldn't be happy just because you're taking up space.

A sense of entitlement is the last mental dead end I want to touch upon. In short, no one in this world owes you shit. You are not entitled to anything: not to wealth, not to sex, not to respect, or even consideration. Everything must be earned. Earning things involves cultivating a talent, developing a skill, learning a trade/profession, i.e. changing yourself so that you have value.

These things also function as your purpose in life: the

Joshua Wetzel

reason(s) that other people will want to give you money, spend time with you, or have sex you. You must have something to offer in exchange, a positive quantity of value they will want a part of. Having that will open doors and create opportunities that you have earned. Having nothing will result in failure, both economically and socially. Choose not to fail. Create a purpose for yourself and pursue it.

Chapter 14
Persona Creation & The Importance of Reputation

Once you have a purpose, you can create a persona and establish a reputation. It doesn't matter who you are at present, you can recreate yourself at will. Some people take the step of moving to a new place, where no one yet knows them, when they decide to create a new persona. The obvious advantage in relocation is all the opportunities that are presented when making new first impressions. Few people (or none) know the old you, so the new you is all they can relate to. Additionally, a relocation means that you can make a radical change, and it won't disrupt your social environment, because one hasn't been established yet. For those who don't want to, or can't relocate, creating a new persona is still possible. It just has to be done more slowly in order to allow others to become used to the new you.

First, pick the persona that you want to step into. It should, optimally, tie back in with whatever purpose you selected in the previous chapter. Additionally, it can be aligned with one of the social types mentioned earlier. For this exercise, I'm going to cover three examples that I've found to be effective for facilitating results: The Expert/Professional, the Gray Person, and finally, the Entertainer. There are practically an infinite number of other persona "types," but if one's ultimate intention aligns with the ultimate goals of toxick magick, i.e. control, and the amplification of the toxick elements within larger systems, then these three are very useful. So, I will go over each of them in a bit more detail.

The Expert/Professional:

This persona involves mastering a skill, trade, or

certification of some type. It can be any role from white collar professions (Doctor, Professor, Scientist, Lawyer, IT Administrator, Salesman, Business Execs of all flavors), to blue collar skilled tradesmen (Plumbers, Electricians, Welders, Carpenters, Brewers, Authors, etc.). You are, for this persona, literally what you do. The toxick magician strives to become the very epitome of whichever is selected. Stepping into this persona usually takes the most time and money from the ones I have selected, but it also has the potential for the greatest impact. This persona is very often a desired and needed component in larger organizations, so to take on one of these roles is an effective way to infiltrate them.

Additionally, the Expert/Professional strives to take on as much responsibility within whatever organization they belong to. This creates dependencies and puts one in the best position to spread corruption when the time comes, but more on that later. In the meantime, acquire an expertise and build an unassailable reputation that you are "the one" that people go to when they need the skills you possess. In time, if you keep your skills sharp, you will have large groups of people figuratively eating out of your hands. This will give you a lot of control over your working environment and basically place everyone else at your mercy.

The Gray Person:

It's good sometimes to go unnoticed, and the persona of the Gray Person takes this skill to its logical extreme. Rather than seeking to stand out like the Professional or the Entertainer, the Gray Person works to make themselves as nondescript as possible. The ultimate goal for this persona is to go unremarked and unnoticed. They are a cog in the machine, a spoke in the wheel, a small part of the larger whole, but a part nonetheless. The anonymity

of this role allows the Gray Person to do damage and then step right back into line without who was responsible being noticed. Done correctly, this can be an effective way to spread corruption within a larger group.

The Gray Person strives to wear clothing which doesn't draw attention to themselves, i.e. whatever is considered stylistically "average" or "plain" (read "blah").[85] At the same time, they refrain from being talkative, saying only what is necessary, nothing more. If they own a car, it's whatever is the most common car to own and is of a bland color. In terms of physical appearance, the goal is to be of an average height and weight if at all possible. It should be noted that these factors are often out of one's control, and you should consider not attempting this persona if you are, for example 6'6"[86] tall. The same could be said for the morbidly obese but to a lesser extent.

The Gray Person doesn't give out details about their lives if it can be avoided. Remaining as anonymous as possible, both online and in real life, is the goal here. Tor browsers, anonymous email accounts, and VPNs are your best bet online, giving personal information out when it's absolutely necessary and never any time else.[87] In conversation, with others the Gray Person doesn't say any more than is absolutely necessary or expected. They never volunteer personal thoughts, feelings, or above all, details about themselves.

The difficulty of this persona is that many people want attention, to stand out, or to be noticed. While getting seen for some personas is very desirable, it's the opposite for the Gray Person. They stick to the shadows in order to get

---

[85] Seeking out an occupation which involves wearing a uniform can help a great deal with this.

[86] Two meters.

[87] Obviously NOT giving your ID to the police when asked is a sure way to GET attention - the opposite of what this persona is trying to achieve.

Joshua Wetzel

things done. Overlooked and unremarkable, they move through the world and leave little to no trace of them having been there. They do enough to get by in any business role and no more. They are the "C" student in the middle of the class, the third shift maintenance worker, the most average of averages.

The reputation of this persona is almost in managing to NOT have a reputation. When their name gets brought up, people should be scratching their heads and wondering, "Who? Oh that guy." Responses like, "I had totally forgotten about them," or, "I can't remember what they looked like," should be your ultimate goal. If public attention suddenly veers your way, you have made a mistake.

The Entertainer:

Related to the Expert/Professional, the Entertainer actively seeks to be the center of attention (and desirability) by mastering a skill. However, unlike the first persona, this role involves using that skill or talent aimed to please the crowd through performance. Once limited to musicians, singers, comedians, theater actors, television, and movie performers, this role has expanded to include online creators in a myriad of forms. Any of these potential pursuits can be undertaken by the toxick magician. The main goal is to achieve fame and notoriety. Once that has been achieved, the medium of whichever talent or skill that was used to reach stardom can be used to spread corruption.

If this persona appeals to the practitioner, there are several considerations to keep in mind before undertaking it. The first thing to keep in mind is that many Entertainer roles require as much work, if not more, than the expert/professional persona. The second consideration is that while many try to become big name entertainers in

142

both mundane or online reality, few succeed to any significant extent. I'm not saying that one can't still have an impact, even if the audience is smaller. I'm just saying, be prepared to not quit your day job. The third consideration is that if you use this persona to inject a toxick rot into the environment, you have to be incredibly subtle while doing so, otherwise you might risk violating the proverb, "don't shit where you eat."

All that being said, this persona has the potential to alter entire genres of entertainment. One need only look at the impact of some of the most famous bands in history. They came along and changed the type of music people consumed (which is huge). To get an idea of how much one entertainer can change reality for large segments of the populace, just recall what happened when the Beatles went on the Ed Sullivan show in 1964. They basically destroyed vaudeville. To be sure, as entertainment for the masses, vaudeville was going out of style at the time, but the Beatles buried alive what was left of it.

The same can be said for the disruption caused by people in online platforms that have overturned classic modes of teaching, getting news, music, DIY repair, and countless other methods of conveying information. If you have an interest, you can find it on the intertoobs. There, you will find a fertile but rather crowded field. Yet, if you have the means, it can be a way to manifest the Entertainer persona.

Once you have chosen a persona, work your way into being it. This will take some time depending on what choice you made above. If you decide to go with the Expert/Professional persona, then you will need to acquire the certifications, education, or skills needed to obtain your objective. This may take weeks, months, or even years, but at least you will have ample time to fashion yourself.

The above applies as well to the Entertainer persona. If you plan on a performance art that involves mastering an instrument or other talent, basic research indicates that you are looking at 20 hours a week for at least a year to get passably good, more if you want to stand out as a skilled performer. Even if you decide to become, say, a YouTuber, that still will involve researching what it took others to become successful and acquiring the necessary recording and editing equipment to create online content.

In terms of the Gray Person, it's practicing all the things to render yourself forgettable and working hard to never break character. As it involves a certain sort of "look," you should consider switching out your wardrobe slowly (this will both be more cost effective and, if you are not in the process of relocating, won't disturb your social circle) while adopting the mannerisms and traits of that particular persona.

After fully moving into your persona, you will need to establish a reputation. Preferably, this reputation will consist of a set of personal traits that will work to your advantage. These traits should be tied to the persona. For example, as mentioned above, it will always work to your benefit in the Expert/Professional persona to be known as "the person to go to" for your particular work. So, cultivate a reputation of professionalism, dependability, honesty, creativity, productiveness, etc. Whatever fits the bill. In terms of the Entertainer, some characteristics might be (but are not limited to) such things as: sociability, creativeness, clarity (if conveying information), experimentalism, innovation, humor (if a comedic type), and expertise regarding the skill that you are entertaining with. Of course, the reputation of the Gray Person is in not having a reputation. Any outstanding qualities should be squashed in an effort to be as unnoticed as possible, and if noticed, thought of as having been vaguely there.

Finally, regardless of the type of reputation you decide

to construct for yourself, once it's constructed, defend it as if your life depends upon it (because it just might). It doesn't matter what type of persona or which traits you have used to fashion a reputation—these must be protected. In the mundane world, image can be everything. If your reputation takes a major hit, you might not be able to recover. People have lost careers, relationships, or even public office once their reputation gets destroyed, so don't allow it to happen.

There are two things to remember along the lines of protecting your reputation: First, if someone is attacking your reputation, never "take the high road" and refuse to respond. When people try to drag you through the mud, you must work hard to counter their narrative. In the absence of any argument or refutation, people will choose to believe the only information available to them. It doesn't matter if that information is false or slanderous, they will believe it as it's the only thing being said. Always refute the attacks of those who smear you, and always go after the character of your enemies in response. Some might judge you negatively for doing so, but they will be in the minority. Get your side of any disagreement in as many ears as possible.

Second, regardless of the persona chosen, be prepared to embrace it or elements of it that might be unexpected. In this, I would like to draw your attention to the tragedy of Jani Lane. He was the lead singer and songwriter for the band Warrant. He came up with the song "Cherry Pie" — the single went double platinum. You would think that would be great, but poor Jani became known as "the Cherry Pie guy" and couldn't shake the association, an association that he couldn't stand and hated. Eventually, he drank himself to death. It didn't have to be that way, he could have embraced being "the Cherry Pie guy", instead he tried to run from it, and that destroyed him.

So, if you find yourself pursuing the Entertainer

persona, keep in mind that you might find yourself permanently pigeonholed by a creation of yours, whether you like it or not. The same could be said for the Expert/Professional—you might create something that will always be associated with you, and you must learn to embrace it. Don't try and reject such things; it won't end well.

Of course, if your reputation gets tarnished, or if you get associated with something you create that you can't stand, you should remember that reinvention of yourself is always an option. Select a new persona, embrace it, and become that new thing. Yes, it will be time consuming, but sometimes one's only option is to burn every bridge, cut every association, and start from scratch. Change your name, your town, and everything about yourself. Ideally, this won't be necessary. If you create a persona, establish a reputation, and defend it vigorously, you won't have to start over.

Chapter 15
The Journaling of Others
(Chapter 1 applied to those closest to you)

Once you have created a purpose for yourself and begun work on a persona, the next step is to gain control over your immediate environment. The first objective is to know as much as possible about those who exist in your personal ecosystem. In order to do this you must master the ability to journal others; your family, friends, associates, coworkers, etc. You should know as much about them as possible. Using the exercises found in the first chapter of this book, modified here, you will be turning the same rigorous attention that you paid to yourself outward instead of inward.

Exercise 1: Who's who in the Zoo?

For any given individual, there are about 150 people with whom they know well enough to comfortably interact. This is commonly referred to as "Dunbar's number[1]," and while it would be an amazing feat of information gathering to be able to completely journal all 150 of these people, it isn't necessary to do so. For most people there is a smaller, more intimate group of family, friends, and coworkers that comprise that person's immediate circle. It is these individuals that comprise your personal zoo so to speak. Journaling them is critical to taking control of your personal ecosystem, so begin by identifying who comprises this group. List the people that make up this group.

I recommend dividing this small group even further into three classifications: home (for immediate family), social (for friends and acquaintances), and work (fellow employees, your boss, etc., or if you are in academia, fellow

147

students, teachers, counselors, etc.). Note, it's not uncommon for there to be overlap. Sometimes, you might be married and work with your spouse, or hang out with coworkers socially, or even find yourself with a chosen, rather than biological, family, etc. The lines between the three subgroups are arbitrary and more an aid to assist in journaling than a hard and fast division.

Once you have identified the members of your three primary ecosystems, take a week to determine how much time you spend with each group and roughly how much time you spend with each person within that group. This will give you a better understanding of who is taking up your time and how they are taking up your time. List the people in each group in descending order, from who takes up the most of your time to who takes up the least. For example:

Home	Social	Work
Spouse	Spouse	Close Coworker
Our Child(ren)	Best Friend	My Boss
Parent(s)	Friend #2	Office Manager
Sibling(s)	Friend#3	Customer
Etc.	Etc.	Customer

You'll begin by journaling the people who take up the majority of your time followed by journaling those who you would consider to have the greatest impact on your time regardless of the actual time they take up, e.g. you might only interact with your boss at work a few times a day, but they might be responsible for giving you a lot of time consuming tasks.

Once you have determined the person from each subgroup (family, social and work) that takes up the most of your time, journal those three individuals. You will be looking to find out as much as possible about them without appearing to be intrusive. There is something of an art to this. Do not ask a ton of questions all at once. Do not ask deeply personal questions. Avoid being obvious. Much of the process involved is mastering the art of paying attention, remembering what you have observed, and being able to discover how other people think and communicate their thoughts about the world as they move through it.

Exercise 2: Journal the primary home person

Depending on your age and social circumstances, the primary home person could be a spouse, a parent, a sibling, a roommate, your best friend, or even your closest neighbor. Ideally, it is someone with whom you are in a relationship with, but it doesn't have to be. I will continue to describe this exercise under the premise that the individual is your significant other, but if it isn't that is fine too.[88] There is no set time limit for these exercises, but you should be able to gather everything you need to know about a person in about a month.

Exercise 2, Step 1: Document what you already know

This step should only take about an hour or two at the most. Sit down and record what you already know about your primary home person. What are you looking to record? Ideally, the list of what you know about them should include:

What is their favorite activity?
What is their favorite food?
Where do they spend the most time?
What are their pet peeves (little things that annoy them)?

---

[88] And if you are a complete hermit when it comes to your home life feel free to skip Exercise 2 and go on to Exercise 3.

What makes them angry? Who do they hate (if anyone)?
What puts them in a good mood?
What are they afraid of (phobias and/or stimuli that cause them to be afraid)?
Who do they spend the most time with?
Who are their friends?
Who are their enemies?
Who are their current and past romantic partners? (if any)
What do they like to do least?
Do they have a particular sexual fetish (yes/no and if yes - what is it?)?
Where do they work (or go to school)?
What do they do for a living?
Do they have a goal/dream that they are trying to reach?
Did they experience any past trauma (if "yes" what was it?)?
What is their proverbial kryptonite (i.e. main weakness)?
What are their strengths (i.e. what do they do well or know well?)?
What do they like least about themselves and what do they like most about themselves?

The above is a typical "master list" that, if answered fully, gives you a complete blueprint of your average human being. It might come as a surprise that you don't currently know all of the answers to the above questions. If you do, great, you can skip the next exercise. If there are holes in your knowledge, move on to the next exercise.

Exercise 2, Step 2: Expand your knowledge of them

In this exercise, you'll carefully fill in any of the missing blanks of your knowledge of the person in question. In order to do this you'll have to do three things: pay attention, maintain outward focus, and remember as much detail as possible. This exercise should generally take about a month, because you do NOT want to pepper any subject, no matter how close they are to you, with a ton of questions — that will just arouse suspicion and will cause just about anyone to shut down and close themselves off to you.

You may be assisted in this exercise if they have an online social presence that you also have access to (and if you don't, acquire it).[89] People reveal all sorts of information about themselves in online media: from blogs, to Facebook statuses, to comments on other peoples' postings or tweets, etc. Whatever is in the public domain, take the time to go through that which you can gain access to. This will probably answer many of the questions that were unanswered in the last step.

In order to find answers to questions that are not already revealed in the public domain, you will have to get them talking about themselves. This is not as hard as it may at first sound. Most people LIKE talking about themselves, we are often our own favorite subject of discussion. Simply asking, "How has your day been? Anything interesting going on?" can often result in a deluge of information. Another more specific trick is to reveal a minor confidentiality (real or made up, it doesn't matter), and this will often elicit a real confidence shared with you in return. For example, you might say something along the lines of: "Ick, I just walked into a spider's web. Spiders really creep me out. Is there ANYTHING as creepy as a really big spider?" They may immediately volunteer their greatest phobia at this point.

---

[89] No. I'm not talking about hacking their account - I'm talking about being on the same social media platforms and seeing what they put there.

This technique can be repeated on other items, i.e. you reveal, say, something you really like to do and then ask them what appeals to them. Again, you don't actually have to really like whatever it is, the goal is getting a response from the target. What you say you like to do is irrelevant. The goal is to get them talking about themselves. Your primary objective here is to be a really great listener. In social engagements, practice saying less and listening more. You don't want to become a mute, you just want those around you to do most of the talking. Keep your focus on them, not on yourself.

Exercise 2, Step 3: Encode and store that information

Once you gain any piece of information, it's important to record it so that you have ready access to it. This will keep you from having to ask people the same questions over and over again. You should have a running file, so to speak, on the most important people around you. Unless you have an eidetic memory, this will have to be written down. Only you should be able to access this repository. A journal kept in a secure location (a locked drawer or safe) or a password protected file on a computer is usually sufficient. That being said, do NOT get sloppy or take it for granted that your location is totally safe. Keys can be misplaced or taken by others and used to gain access; passwords can be hacked; etc. I recommend taking the added step of creating a cipher to be used when recording information about others. That way, there is an added level of security. There is plenty of information online about creating ciphers. However, if you are a dinosaur like me, you might contrive to create your own. I've included a simple, old one of mine in image 1 on the next page:

Image 1:

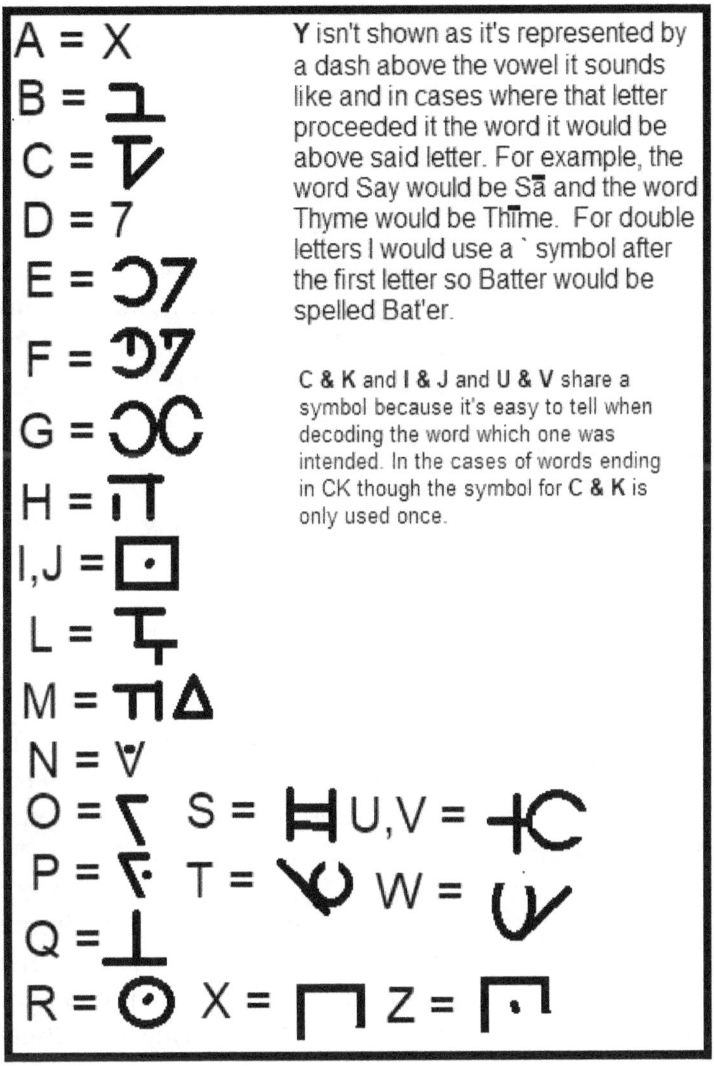

A = X

B = (symbol)

C = (symbol)

D = 7

E = (symbol)

F = (symbol)

G = (symbol)

H = (symbol)

I,J = (symbol)

L = (symbol)

M = (symbol)

N = (symbol)

O = (symbol)   S = (symbol)   U,V = (symbol)

P = (symbol)   T = (symbol)   W = (symbol)

Q = (symbol)

R = (symbol)   X = (symbol)   Z = (symbol)

Y isn't shown as it's represented by a dash above the vowel it sounds like and in cases where that letter proceeded it the word it would be above said letter. For example, the word Say would be Sā and the word Thyme would be Thīme. For double letters I would use a ` symbol after the first letter so Batter would be spelled Bat'er.

C & K and I & J and U & V share a symbol because it's easy to tell when decoding the word which one was intended. In the cases of words ending in CK though the symbol for C & K is only used once.

By combining a cipher with a secure location (in my case, it was a locked desk drawer), it is possible to come close to having your journaling be 100% secure from any prying eyes.

Exercise 4, Step 4: Memorization

The information you have gathered won't do you any good if you can't recall it, so take the necessary time to memorize key things about the person. This can be done via repetition of facts regarding them until you have that information down cold. One trick is to create a mnemonic device[90] using the first letter of each thing you discovered about them. You then memorize that mnemonic device. If you have access to a computer as of the writing of this book, there is even an online tool that can generate it for you: Mnemonic Generator. mnemonicgenerator.com

Conclusion: Some final thoughts and a recap

For anyone you are journaling, the following techniques can be useful:

1) Say as little as possible, let anyone you're with do the majority of the talking.

2) Be friendly and maintain a pleasant disposition. This puts people at ease, and people at ease are more likely to reveal truths about themselves that they would otherwise hide.

3) Reveal harmless "secret" information about yourself (even make things up) to tell to the person that you are journaling—often, sharing an essentially fake or minor confidence will result in them sharing something significant about themselves to you.

4) Match the views and opinions of the person you are

---

[90] A pattern of letters, ideas, or associations that assists in remembering something.

journaling. This will also work to open them up more to reveal aspects of themselves, as you will appear to be a kindred spirit.

5) If possible, be a source of pleasure. This ties back into the first tactic; if you are enjoyable to be around, people will want you around, and the more you are around them, the more they will share about themselves.

6) Never offend or make a joke at the expense of the person you are journaling. If you do, you risk them clamming up and mentally withdrawing.

7) Befriend a close friend of the person you are journaling, if possible. Often times, they will be willing to relate stories and information about your target that you wouldn't be able to get directly from them. Of course, try to be subtle about it—the last thing you would want is them going to your target later and mentioning that you were asking a lot of questions about them.

8) Befriend a former friend of the person you are journaling, if possible. Former friends often make the most bitter enemies and are usually happy to spill any dirt they might have on your target. They are also very unlikely to reveal that you were asking questions.

9) Observe them online, if that is an option. Don't reveal that you're observing them online, but definitely do if you can—join the same groups online, the same forums or what not, participate as little as possible, but observe as much as you can.

Once you've journaled the primary person from each of your three groups, you can journal additional people in your home, social, and work groups using the same

Joshua Wetzel

techniques. Knowing as much about the people around you is crucial to success in the next chapter. The more information you gather, the easier it will be going forward. It's a cliche that "knowledge is power," but when it comes to people, it very much holds true; the more knowledge you have of someone, the more potential power you have over them. The less you know about them, the less power.

Chapter 16
The Control of Others

Using the exercises in the previous chapters, you've learned the ways to control yourself physically, emotionally, and mentally. Additionally, you should have mastered meditation, states of Trance, and Ekstasis. Finally, you have discovered a purpose for yourself, grasped the importance of creating avenues of manifestation, internalized the techniques of strategic magick, and gathered (journaled) information on those in your home, social, and work/school environments. In essence, you've completed the extension of personal control over yourself. The next three chapters will outline how to extend that control over other individuals, groups, and organizations, with the final chapter discussing ways of corrupting them.

What does it mean to have control over others? Specifically, it means getting what you want in a given set of circumstances. In other words, it involves those around you working in your favor, rather than against you. For this to occur, it would behoove you to ensure that people possess a positive disposition towards you, regardless of the environment you find yourself in. They should not only want to help you, but they should believe that it's in their best interest to do so. Failing that, they will understand that working against you will be more detrimental to them than to you.

This chapter will go over techniques used to control others that have been found to work. In addition to the techniques listed, I'll also provide example scenarios to provide a more complete picture. In the end, mix and match whatever techniques appear to apply to a given situation.

Technique 1: Keep Things Private

As you probably discovered in the process of journaling others, the primary weakness of just about everyone is the ease in which they give up information: personal likes/dislikes, what their plans are, what they hope to accomplish, their regrets, what they think about other people, etc. Sometimes, they go so far as to wear their emotions on their proverbial sleeves. It's all there for the taking (or asking) if you use the techniques in the preceding chapter. Combine journaling yourself along with dealing with others, and you'll have the advantage in just about any situation, if done effectively. In other words, you will have followed the advice of Sun Tzu's "Art of War" — " If you know the enemy and know yourself, you need not fear the result of a hundred battles." This is a great advantage to hold, to be sure.

This can also be taken one step further by making sure that, while you know as much as there is to know about the people around you, the same cannot be said of you from their perspective. Oh, they might THINK they know you. After all, you will probably have revealed some things about yourself in the process of winning their confidence and opening them up. However, if you were careful, then what you did reveal was either untrue or of such a trivial nature as to have no value in terms of information.

In your interactions with others, never reveal your plans until either they have borne fruit or have reached a stage at which nothing can be done to stop them. This is particularly important when it comes to situations in which you may be in competition for something (or someone). It's easiest to win a race when you're the only participant that knows that a race is happening at all.

Definitely remain quiet when it comes to long range plans, dreams, and ambitions. If others don't know what you're going for, they won't be able to put obstacles in your way. The only few who should be "in the know" are the rare individuals that are necessary for you to reach your goals. Preferably, they won't be close friends or associates. Rather, they might be some form of mentor, teacher, or financial resource that you can draw from. Even with these people, only reveal what is absolutely necessary. Don't elaborate.

Never reveal what you truly feel or think about other people, even when pressed. Keep these opinions to yourself. There are gossips in just about every group, types who love to find out what you REALLY think of some mutual friend or acquaintance. They do so in order to rat you out and possibly damage or destroy any meaningful relationship you might have had. They might also simply do it for the love of stirring up drama. Deprive them of any ammunition by not having an opinion. More specifically, do not reveal the opinion that you actually have.

In any interaction always say little and listen a lot. This will increase the amount of information that you have while depriving those around you of any dirt on you. Keep any social media presence to a bare minimum. Never open up about anything significant online, especially regarding anything which could be viewed as a weakness. Superficiality is the goal here. Present enough to gather information, yet distant enough to keep your own secrets secret.

Apart from the trivial, only share information when you achieve success. You will still appear to be playing the social media game while never truly giving away what you are doing. The only thing people should ever be presented with is a fait accompli. This will rob them of agency and keep them from thwarting your plans. As alluded to above, rivals and enemies won't be able to throw obstacles in your path if they don't know the route you are traveling.

Technique 2: Dirty Little Secrets

Once you have successfully journaled a number of individuals, you will (most likely) have uncovered a number of things about them which they had been keeping private. Of these items, two are key to having control over them. The first are items/secrets that can be used to blackmail. The second is hidden fetishes, desires, addictions, or fantasies that they keep private. Let's go over each in turn.

If you uncover something (an affair, illegal activity, etc.) that your target has been keeping under wraps, you have the potential to blackmail them. However, I recommend only using blackmail as a last resort and in circumstances in which you have no other way to get them to do what needs to be done. Using blackmail as a technique can very easily backfire; there are too many things that can go wrong. This is especially true if you and the victim are frequently involved in each other's lives.

First, if they trusted you (hence, how you learned of their secret) that trust is blown. Except to keep the information about themselves from ever reaching the light of day, they won't ever trust you again, and they will never willingly be a resource that you can exploit. Odds are, they will now be your enemy and will work against you. That hassle alone isn't worth whatever you might get out of the blackmail. Second, the longer you keep their secret, the more you are implicated in the keeping of it. When it does come out, the blowback may also damage you and negate any benefit that you are deriving from blackmailing the person in question. Third, they may call your bluff and challenge you to reveal that information. This combines the worst of the aforementioned bad outcomes.

As mentioned above, blackmail is only useful in circumstances when you have no other option. Maybe through a third party you discovered sensitive information about someone who was already in an adversarial role against you. If they are currently your enemy, you don't have anything to lose vis-a-vis that person, so blackmailing them becomes more feasible. It still might result in a bad outcome in terms of the second and third negative outcomes listed above, but at least you won't risk losing a friend (unless it's the person who got you that information, so also bad).

That being said, blackmail information that is obtained regarding an enemy has one potentially positive hidden benefit. It might allow you to turn an opponent into an ally. After all, you are in on their "secret", if you are planning on keeping it with no perceivable benefit rebounding to you the subject in question might begin to see you in a more positive light. After all, you could have destroyed some aspect of their life by making it public but chose not to. In essence you are now their co-conspirator. They might turn into your bestest buddy overnight, but they might stop being your worst nightmare and that can only help you and your situation.

It is more useful to discover a person's desires, fantasies, addictions or hidden fetishes. Things that they want that you can provide them or exchange with them to get their assistance or, at the very least, keep them from getting in the way of your own objectives. As mentioned in the journaling of others chapter information of this type can be obtained by listening more and saying less on the one hand and by revealing small (or fake) confidences that illicit real secrets on the other.

The trick here is managing the quid pro quo[91] between you and the target. There is no point, for example, in just providing an addict with their drug of choice if you get nothing in return from it. The person in question has to

---

[91] Latin for "like for like" - usually an equal trade, but in our case hopefully more for less.

have something that you want or need in exchange. Or they must be capable of performing some task for you in order to justify you feeding their habit. So, before plying them with what they want, make sure that you know what you want to get first and that they know what is expected of them.

In the right circumstances this leverage can be used again and again often resulting in a symbiotic relationship in which each party is getting what they want. They only caution here might be to not rely too heavily on this technique. It's effective but also involves you doing or providing something in exchange. Optimally, what you are providing to them is less than what you are getting out of them. If it isn't, you need to stop. Only feed the desires of others if it benefits you in some way. Otherwise, you risk becoming nothing more than a conduit for what they want. Make sure that you are getting real value (whether through favors, money or work performed) out of them.

Technique 3: Build Emotional Relationships

To get others to want to help you reach your goals (or at the very least not impede you from reaching them) you have to, in effect, seduce them into wanted to help you. In order to do that you have to develop an emotional rapport with them. They have to come to like you and thus be motivated to help you. The apex of success in this technique is marked by them seeing their assistance of you as their idea when, in fact, you seduced them to that way of thinking.

In every meaningful interaction pay attention to, and match how they frame the world.[92] If they are primarily visual then remember to use the visual frame set of

---

[92] Refer back to Section 1, Chapter 6 "Mental Control" if you need a refresher.

terminology and the same for the auditory and kinesthetic frames. People naturally like those who appear to understand them and using the same framing will provide the illusion that you both frame the world the same way and thus understand each other. The same goes for if they highlight sameness or look for differences to relate to things and experiences. Again, subtly match how they communicate using similar but not identical words.

If you have had the opportunity to journal them properly then you may have picked up on their political, religious and social preferences. It's not necessary to agree 100% with every view, however, you should always hint that you do agree, or that you do see or feel as they do. When you appear as everything to everyone you will know you have succeeded. In doing so you will have everyone believing that on some level they have a special relationship with you. Whether that be as casual associates, friends or lovers really doesn't matter.

Avoid arguing at all costs. The points scored demonstrating you were right and they were wrong will only cause resentment on their part and rob you of a resource. You don't have to agree with everyone, just avoid disagreement. If you slip up and say something that is diametrically opposed to their worldview, and they catch you out on that, take the time to allow them to "persuade" you to their way of thinking. This will make them feel good about themselves and they will like you more in the process.

I will add a caveat here. There are those with views so extreme that you'll only damage yourself and your reputation by associating with them. You must constantly weigh any benefit derived from an association with any negative consequence of that association. Some individuals are too costly for you to be seen with. Keep them out of your life. If having them in your life risks alienating all of your other friends, or puts your job at risk, or adversely impacts your chosen family, etc. Ghost them.

Technique 4, Maintain the Initiative

In order to control those around you that may, themselves, be very driven and productive people you have to maintain the initiative with regard to them - i.e. they should be reacting, whether they know it or not, to your machinations and not the other way around. Keeping one step ahead of everyone else will give you time to prepare for situations before they arise and additionally will give you breathing space and time to react to unexpected events. As these will happen.

There are three ways to establish and retain the initiative in your interactions with others: First, determine what you want out of any given circumstance in advance. In other words, plan ahead. Don't lurch from task to task in a permanently reactive mode. Get up early and figure out what you want from the day, week, month or season and lay out the steps to get there.[93] Second, determine what is in your way and also what resources and/or can be used to facilitate you reaching your objective. Third, when you do decide to act, act decisively, obtain your objective, and then consolidate your gains lest you risk squandering them. Collectively this technique is known as "planning all the way to the end." Let's go over each of these steps in a little more detail below.

Scenario: You may find yourself working in a low paying job with little prospects for advancement and your goal is either a promotion with more pay or a new job entirely making more money and with some opportunity for advancement. You have to ask yourself some brutally honest questions. You have to journal yourself. Why am I

---

[93] In short, always have a plan of action regardless of if it's for the day, the week, a month or a season.

in this role? Was this the best that I could hope for? Basically, how did I wind up here? What am I doing that is holding myself back? Are there external forces hindering my progress?

Naming things gives you power over them, identify what is in your way. Maybe there wasn't any other job available. Maybe you lack (at present) the education to obtain a better job. Maybe economic circumstances forced you to take the first job that came along. Maybe you've just always done just enough to get by and nothing more. Maybe there is nothing in your current location beyond what you have.

Next is more information gathering. Maybe there is an opportunity to advance in your current job but you just never asked your boss or another higher up what it took to get there. I've found that, if approached in the right way, people who have been successful in a given field will straight up TELL you what they did to get to where they are at. It's that simple. Or, if you know you want to seek opportunity elsewhere, seek out those who have excelled in what you are interested in pursuing and straight up ask them what they did to achieve results. If that isn't available there are resources online which can be investigated. Again, the successful love talking about themselves. Mine their confessions for possible routes to success.

Then once you've figured out what you need to do - do it. Maybe it's long nights studying, maybe it's saving up and moving to a new town, maybe it's working twice as hard as the bastard next to you, it could be any and all of these things or something else entirely. For example, in some corporations you get ahead by volunteering for more work, letting those above you know you are interested in advancement and acquiring new knowledge to insure competence in your new role.

Once you've reached your goal consolidate your gains. Napoleon Bonaparte is famous for saying: "The greatest danger occurs at the moment of victory." This is especially true when your success has come at the cost of someone else. Be prepared for blowback. If you have ruffled any feathers make an attempt to soothe them. For example, perhaps you beat someone else out for a better position at work. If possible, assure them that it was just dumb luck that they picked you. Or reveal an (false) insecurity that you're worried that you will not be up to the new responsibility and ask them if you can count on their expertise and advice. It might not always work, you might have made an implacable foe, but it's worth the effort to try and neutralize them as a threat. If all else fails, set your next goal as getting them fired.

How does all of the above play into controlling others? Simple, by heading determinedly in one direction, others are forced to react to your initiative rather than taking control themselves. The vast majority of people in your environment are, at the most basic level, just trying to avoid pain and maximize pleasure. In short, they are doing just enough to get by and are drifting, rudderless, through their lives. Don't just drift along with them. Pick a direction/goal and head towards it.

Once obtained, set another goal and then another so on and so forth. They don't have to all be lofty goals, they can be simple, short-term objectives too. If you have the energy you can even pursue more than one goal at a time, the process of doing so is the meta objective here. Retain the initiative through always remaining the proactive individual in your environment. Others will be forced to react to you or get out of your way. And that is where you want them, on the back foot. Keeping them there is done by continuing to drive forward.

Technique 5, Color and/or limit the choices presented to others.

One of the most frustrating, day to day annoyances is

people in your immediate environment failing to make decisions. Everything from "What do you want to do tonight?" or "Where should we go to dinner?" to larger questions regarding major life decisions such as "Should we have children?" or "Should we get married?" or "Should I go back to school?" etc. Nine times out of ten, unless you yourself are taking the initiative you will be met with hemming and hawing, evasion and indecision. If you are tired of this, there is a simple solution. Color and/or limit the choices that you are presenting to others. (Also mention using too many choices to paralyze)

First, never even ask an open-ended question. For example, don't ask "Where should we go to dinner?" - that will only engender unhelpful responses, instead phrase it as: "Let's go out to dinner, I'm thinking either Sushi or Pho? Which do you prefer?" note that you've already gained control of the situation in that you've given options that you happen to want but left them with the illusion that they are making a meaningful decision. Second, you can take this technique one step further by coloring the choice presented. "Let's go out to dinner, I'm thinking either Sushi or Pho, but, you know, we just had Sushi last week? What do you think? We both like Pho after all." - Again, not only are you presenting two items that you'd be happy with, giving them the illusion that they have a say in the matter but you're ALSO setting it up so that there really is only one choice, the one you want.

This does involve you having a plan to begin with and that isn't bad. It's good to figure out what you want before you even interact with another person. As mentioned above, start each day with a plan. This will give you the initiative, time to figure out what you want to say to them and when. Thus leaving you in control of the situation. Your control is cemented by ensuring that those you interact with only ever make decisions based on the options you present. And this can work in a variety of situations.

The technique also applies to larger life questions such as: "Should we buy a house?" - if you want to buy a house with your partner you ask the question one way and if you don't you ask it another. If you do you ask: "I was thinking it might make sense for us to buy a house. Should we do it? Property can be a good investment and with renting we're just flushing money down the toilet every month as opposed to paying down a mortgage, where, in the end, we're really paying ourselves. What do you think?" If you don't you ask: "Do you think we should buy a house? The housing market is so volatile these days and there's no telling it would go up or down in value. Plus, instead of the landlord having to pay for things when they break it would be on us. And then there's all that yardwork, maintenance and shoveling snow. What do you think?" In both cases the odds are that they will select the outcome you want as you've colored the choice in such a way that to select the other one would imply that they are making a mistake.

This method can also be flipped on its head. If you want to paralyze someone present them with multiple choices. Specifically give them more than three. The human mind has a tendency to freeze up when there is just too much to choose from and no one option outshines any of the others. So, for example, if you don't want to go out for dinner suggest more than three places, rapidly and then end with something like "Or we could skip all the hassle and crowds and order in tonight." Presented with too many choices, but given the escape hatch of just ordering something delivered, most people will opt for what appears to be the easiest option.

Technique 6, Never be a White Knight / Avoid Human Drains

If you want to be in control of those around you, you must also avoid being controlled. As you work to establish an ever-widening sphere of personal control be aware that there are those who pull the trick of dominating others through weakness. Three of the most insidious forms that manipulators of this type take are that of the "damsel in distress"[94], "the personal project" and "the perpetually broken". These three categories of leeches should be assiduously avoided. If someone you know falls into one of these categories already, ghost them. Cut them out of your life completely. They only exist to take and they will do so until there is nothing left of you.

"The Damsel in Distress"

No matter how desirable or attractive some people seem at first glance, never get involved with anyone who doesn't have their proverbial shit together or at the very least is on the way to getting it together on their own. In other words, always steer clear of anyone who is clearly a "hot mess". If someone appears to be in need of saving they will often be in distress because of their own bad decisions. In other words, no matter how much time, love and money you throw their way they will never get any better and when you are sucked dry of resources they will move on to the next "rescuer".

But how can they be spotted before you become emotionally entangled? One way is that they will often have a trail of bitter ex-lovers and ex-friends who will warn you off. Listen to their side of the story and try and picture yourself in their shoes vis-a-vis the person you are trying to "save". Even just one bitter ex should be enough to make it clear that you should stay well away. Although it's not unusual for ex partners to have some complaints, after all, the relationship failed and someone must be to blame. Take heed of what they say and especially pay

---

[94] And to be fair, the "damsel" in this case can be male, female, non-binary, etc.

attention if they mention that the way things went wrong was the same as the way things went wrong for the person before them too.

"The Personal Project"

We all know of people who fell short of their potential. They could have been really great at something but never managed to make it. How wonderful it would be for them, and you if they could be supported and nurtured in such a way to make that come about. Like the "damsel in distress" this person will, in all likelihood act as a drag on you and your own ambitions. Avoid becoming this person's mentor, guide or support mechanism. The time and attention you waste on them could have been spent on pursuing your own goals and happiness.

These people are easy enough to spot. They are often unemployed or underemployed. If employed at all they do the bare minimum to get by and nothing more. If you find one of them in your circle of associates you don't have to cut them off or out completely. Just minimize your exposure to them - don't offer them support or advice, let someone else do that. You focus instead on those who can benefit you and your situation. Leave the personal project types for others to waste their time on. Optimally, if you have a friend/competitor you can throw this person their way. Let them get bogged down trying to push them to achieve anything of note.

"The Perpetually Broken"

These come in three sub-flavors: The mentally broken, the emotionally broken and the physically broken. It's not uncommon for the former two to fall into the category of "the damsel in distress". Often the damsel in question got that way because of poor coping strategies adopted to deal with stressful or traumatic situations. They might be habitual liars, be physically, verbally or emotionally

170

abusive. Or they might be addicted to some form of drug[95]. It is unfortunate that bad things happened to them. However, you shouldn't be dragged down by their tragedy. You cannot save them and you cannot fix them. Do not let them infect you with their misery. Below they are described in a bit more detail to give you an idea of who to avoid.

The physically broken suffer from one or more chronic conditions, although this isn't what puts them in this category. There are many people who have managed to create worthwhile lives for themselves even with the pain and/or handicaps that they have to deal with. The physically broken ones are those who are NOT coping. They will consume as much of your time and resources as they can so that someone else is also burdened. Don't assume this role. Let someone else deal with them.

The mentally broken category covers people suffering from a debilitating mental illness. Leave them to the professionals. Stay well clear. The minute it's clear that someone you know is, in fact, fucking crazy, get the hell away from them. Sooner or later there will be some sort of disaster that they will be at the center of. Get out of the blast zone and stay out of it. It is a fact that some types of "crazy" can be contagious. Specifically, "Folie à deux"[96] which can occur when you indulge someone in their madness and subsequently amplify it and go down with them when destruction comes. As a side note, with a particularly charismatic individual madness can spread to entire groups. These are often termed "cults" and should be avoided as well. Don't be convinced of your own abilities to the point that you think you can ever infiltrate a cult and take it over. I can assure you that the odds are pretty well set that you will be the one controlled and

[95] To quote off the Ministry album "Psalm 69": Never trust a junkie.
[96] French for "madness for two"

exploited by the group rather than the other way around.

The emotionally broken covers, as mentioned above, individuals who are physically, verbally or emotionally abusive. They have never achieved the ability to control their emotions and if you are exposed to them for too long they will negatively impact your ability to stay in control of your own feelings. Though some emotionally broken people can temporarily pass for "normal" in an average social setting they will, at some point, lash out when stressed. They will either run you down verbally (name calling, unfair criticism, etc.), emotionally (crying, screaming, usually with phrases beginning with "You never.....!" or "You always ...!" or physically by striking you. Never respond in kind. Distance yourself from these types as soon as they reveal themselves to be truly the emotional basket cases that they are. And if you are physically struck? Pack your literal or figurative bags and get the fuck away from them as soon as it is safe to do so.

Endnote: Some Final Thoughts regarding the Making of Plans

I talked above about making plans and that one should have a plan for the day, the week, the month and the season. I did this being well aware of the many, many very true sayings regarding the hazards of planning such as: "If you want to make the gods laugh, come up with a plan." or "The best laid schemes o' mice an' men / Gang aft agley."[97] or even the one military minds are fondest of: "No plan survives contact with the enemy." These sayings speak to the unpredictable events and situations which can derail even a well thought out plan. And yes, nothing can be done to prevent the totally unexpected, but a lot can be done to correct for the reasonably expected. After all, every

[97] Robert Burns: "To a Mouse" 1785

car comes with a spare tire. When you make plans, you should always attach to them a metaphorical spare tire.

The form it takes can be any number of things depending on the plan in question. Perhaps you had plans to go out but these were cancelled unexpectedly, have a backup in mind beforehand. Or maybe you were going to work through a task during the day but something at work malfunctioned and you were either unable to do what you had in mind or were the one responsible for putting out the fire. Have a fallback time to work on the task already set. This also holds true for things like working out. If you miss a day, no problem, always be prepared to simply do it the next day. The key to successful planning is not only having a plan but having a flexible plan.

If you make a plan that lacks flexibility and something out of the blue thwarts your plan you will probably feel like a failure. Don't allow that to happen. Implant the potential for variation into any scheme so that if the first and best outcome doesn't take place there is a second or even a third fallback option to reset to. That way potential failure will be turned into success. Inflexibility is the only way to lose when it comes to planning, flexibility results in there being many ways to win.

Chapter 17
Organizational Control

There are many types of organizations in the world — from the very small, like a local homeowner's association, up to large international companies containing hundreds of thousands of people. Regardless of their size all organizations share some elements in common: one or more individuals in positions of authority, critical members that do most of the actual "work" to keep things running, and a semi-constant flow of internal politics. Eventually, you can mold the environment of the organization to your liking by using a number of strategies. Taken to extremes, the strategies below will result in you controlling it entirely. Used judiciously, at the very least, you can ensure that your presence within the organization is comfortable and secure. For example, if it's a corporation, you can work yourself into a position of solid income and minimum workload. How far you take it is entirely up to you.

Strategy 1: Never upstage or fight with your boss; emulate them

I once had an associate who was a skilled technician. They held a set of mechanical certifications and knowledge of how things worked in their field that was second to none. However, they were eventually completely unemployable and are now on track to die in poverty. This is a pathetic and entirely avoidable outcome. Why did it occur? They ignored this strategy throughout their entire adult life. They were constantly at loggerheads with their boss(es). Gregarious, easy going, and extremely likeable when it came to their coworkers and friends, they never thought to charm the person signing their paychecks. This resulted in termination after termination until no company was left that was willing to hire such a "bad apple."

Never risk alienating the person who determines your continued existence within an organization. Doing so is to risk professional suicide. Never directly contradict them (especially in front of others) or upstage them by demonstrating that you are either more knowledgeable, talented, or skilled than they are. Any momentary satisfaction derived by doing so is not worth it in the long run. You will have made them resent you or worse, made them jealous of you, thus turning them against you. Instead, work in the entirely opposite direction; keep them on your side.

How do you best accomplish this? First, journal them. Understand what they like and don't like, their political leanings, their hobbies, pursuits, and interests. As mentioned before, people love talking about themselves. If you can get your boss talking, pay close attention to what is important to them. Odds are they will readily share this information, as its basic and mundane. It's just who they are. In sharing this information, they are giving you the keys to staying on their good side.

Second, emulate them to the best of your ability. People like those that are like themselves, at least to a limited extent. The more they see themselves in you, the more they will both like you and want you to succeed. Are they a bit of a curmudgeon? Then be one too. Are they generally happy, outgoing, and of good humor most days? Then try and be that too. Seriously, laugh at their jokes, take their side in any decision or disagreement, show sympathy and support during moments of adversary. Demonstrate that you are like them and on their side, and they will subconsciously come to think of you as being on THEIR side.

Third, always say yes.[98] Consider adopting a variation

[98] With the exception of unwanted sexual advances.

of the following mantra if your boss ever asks you to sum up your personal work ethic: "I go where you tell me to go. I do what you tell me to do, and I do it to the best of my ability." You might be surprised at how few people in an organization approach their superiors this way. For many bosses, to get their employees to do even the most straightforward (or easy) thing is like pulling teeth.[99] Instead of compliance, there is always pushback and resistance. Don't risk being seen as a roadblock between your boss and what they want.

Finally, when you do something outstandingly well, make sure that they get some or all of the credit. Make your boss look good in front of their peers and their own superiors, and they will, in turn, always have your back. This is done by framing your achievements with caveats like: "Well, I never would have been able to do it without so-and-so's idea/advice/input/support," etc. You both might know deep down that it was all you, but by sharing a bit of credit with your boss, you not only help them, you help yourself.

By being fairly like them in attitude and temperament, dependable to them when needed, and reflecting positively on them to others, you can insure your position. Not only that, if you desire advancement, you will have them as a political ally. If you don't require or desire advancement, you will at least ensure that your situation isn't under constant threat. This allows you to focus on other things than just "the job" or "the club" or "the group."

Strategy 2: Establish a good reputation and protect it with your life

How you are viewed within an organization is actually

---

[99] The same holds true in hierarchical social groups and most other organizations.

more important than what you do or don't do on a day-to-day basis. Depending on your personal strengths, you should work to establish a good reputation around what you do best. It can be anything that's worthy of respect. Those who, for example, establish a reputation as a hard worker can, once that reputation is established, focus their attention elsewhere. In other words, once you've built a reputation as a hard worker, ironically, you don't have to work that hard anymore.

Others might work to be the "go to" person for something valued within the organization. This will ensure that when something is needed regarding something, people will come to you first and foremost; you are the expert. If you are, say, the master of a specific technology or skill, make sure that you establish a reputation as being THE one that people should go to when it's needed. This will also result in people being dependent on you. When you create that dependency, you have secured your place in the organization. More on dependency is covered below.

Another possible useful reputation to engender, with regard to being in control within an organization, is that of "social know-it-all" for lack of a better term. In every group, there is usually someone who is the first to know: an expert at ferreting out information from others. Often they are the ones who have mastered the skill of networking (see below). By being socially plugged-in to multiple sub-groups within an organization, the "social know-it-all" is perpetually ahead of the curve. If people know that you are the one that is "in the know," they will often spill the beans on new and/or confidential information which may be crucial to staying on top of events. In other words, they will take it for granted that you already know, even if you don't—your reputation thus helps in this regard.

Whatever reputation you do establish, remember that

keeping it is supremely important. If your reputation is damaged — say, someone comes to believe that you are lazy or a liar or clueless, or untrustworthy, etc. — it can be fatal to your control of the organization. So, keep your guard up, and know that you must periodically burnish your reputation by doing a bit of work to maintain it. If you don't, and your reputation crumbles, you'll be forced to move on to some other company or group. In extreme cases, you'll have to move out of town. As that's a major hassle to be avoided, maintain a good reputation.

Strategy 3: Create dependencies

As mentioned above, there is value in establishing the reputation of being THE expert on something or being THE person to go to when things need to get done. If done correctly, this will create dependencies; others will be forced to rely on you. When they do, you are in a position to get something in exchange for your help. You have, in essence, established control over those around you by them needing what you provide.

Parallels can be found to this in the form of drug addiction. If someone is an addict, and you are the supplier, you have control of them.[100] The dealer can extract resources (money or favors) in exchange for providing the drug of choice. An expert or master of a particular skill can extract resources similarly, so assume that role if possible. When people come to you for your expertise, use their need to extract what you want from them. If you don't need anything from them immediately, make sure that they understand that they are in your debt. You may need them at a later date and having them indebted to you turns them into a resource.

Personally, I always keep tabs on what I've done for

---

[100] Please note that I am NOT recommending becoming a drug dealer.

whom and when. It makes it easier to turn to them when I am in need. Reminding them that they owe me facilitates me getting what I want out of them. If someone you have placed in your debt fails to repay you (either in money, favors, or what you want to get out of them), refrain from helping them in future. They are a poor investment of your time, skill, money, or expertise. Never proverbially throw good money after bad. Those who are dependent on you should have some value to you.

The ultimate goal with this strategy is to place yourself, like a spider, at the center of a web of interdependencies and obligations. The more that people come to you to get things done, the more you can get done in turn through them. The more you can get done, the more power you ultimately have over the group.

Strategy 4: Never isolate yourself; network

Within any organizational structure, the best-connected individuals are inevitably the ones who are in control of the organization or some facet of it. Some of the most powerful people in the world are the ones with the most connections. So, create as many connections as possible. They don't all have to be deeply intimate; they just have to exist. You should never be part of just one social group within an organization or isolated to just one department. You must strive to build bridges to as many subsets within a larger group as possible.

For example, within large corporations, there are often opportunities to volunteer to participate with various groups that are not strictly career specific. There might be an emergency responder team or an auditing team, etc. Get on those and cement a good reputation with the other participants. Within your own area, always volunteer to take on more; get your fingers into as many pies as possible. This will allow you to have visibility into many areas and thus be able to act quicker as situations arise.

Additionally, getting known and well-liked is insurance against being booted out of any group. The better your reputation and the more you are liked and respected, the more mistakes you can make and get away with. The less, the fewer. The isolated, anti-social people in any group are often not very far from being kicked out. So, push yourself to engage with the others in the company or organization as much as possible. Obviously, you will have to balance socializing with being productive. This will keep your reputation intact.

While networking, avoid doing the following: Giving bad news, cynicism, expressing radical ideas or opinions, being argumentative and angry, complaining too much, bragging, or expressing any form of extreme emotion. I'll expand a bit on those now in more detail.

Never, ever (if you can manage it) be the bearer of bad news. Whenever possible, have it conveyed by someone else, unless there is no other option. As much as people say, "don't shoot the messenger," it is an aspect of human nature to at least partially associate the news with the news giver. Avoid that association. Conversely speaking, when there is good news to share, strive to be the one to deliver it first whenever possible. This will set up the connection between you and good news. This will increase your appeal, and people who are liked are the likeliest to get assistance/their way/rewarded/etc.

Don't be the group cynic. A biting, insightful comment might be good for a laugh now and then, but as an overall personality, the cynic is ultimately counterproductive if you are trying to establish control over a group. People will get really tired of that attitude really fast, and it will impede your networking. People avoid the cynical and the depressed, so refrain from being either.

Refrain from expressing radical opinions or notions. You are certainly free to have them, but in a group environment, keep them to yourself. Should controversial topics come up, align your view with the group majority or, if you have a superior, align your views with theirs. People tend to like those that think as they do far more than those whose views are strange and outlandish. This practice also fits with the tactic of keeping as much about yourself possible private. Blend in with the group outwardly; think however you like inwardly.

Never argue. Never lose your temper. No one is ever won over to your way of thinking by arguing with them and much less so by shouting at them. By acting confrontationally, people will avoid you or even dread the thought of being in the same room with you. In addition, if you do argue with someone and humiliate them, you risk them holding a grudge against you. Finally, it cuts down the probability that they will be a resource for you down the road. Avoid arguing with and alienating those around you. The alienated will refuse to help you, put roadblocks in your way, or even actively work to undermine you. Keep as many people on your side as possible.

Avoid bragging and showboating. People resent those who wave their accomplishments in their faces. Worse than that, they come to envy them. Succeed, but go about it in a subdued fashion. Actions speak louder than words in this regard. If you do happen to be extremely talented, don't blow your own trumpet. That being said, people should know that you at least have a trumpet. This is done through accomplishing tasks, reaching goals, etc. but without shouting about them from the rooftop. People will respect you for being low-key in this way, and that will also bolster your reputation.

As with rage mentioned above, stay away from extreme emotions in a group setting. Specifically, avoid crying in front of other people. This can be difficult in extremely stressful situations, but you must stay focused and not give in to the desire to burst into tears.[101] If you are going to break down do it when you can have some privacy. No one wants to associate with a person who constantly is on the verge of bawling like an infant so don't do it.

Strategy 5: Keep your hands clean

As you progress in taking control within a group, you will occasionally engage in hostile actions against adversaries that you might have made within the organization. You might have made a mistake and created an enemy, or you might find that you want something, but another person is in your way. In dealing with them, it's important to keep your hands clean. Never openly attack. Use the techniques discussed in the chapter on strategic magick. If you have managed to effectively create a number of interdependencies and have succeeded at networking, you will be able to act through others rather than directly.

In the end, let someone else be your hatchet man. Do not be openly vicious to the person you are targeting in any way. If other people perceive you as someone who openly goes after other people, this can backfire. Your allies, resources, and people who you have nothing against should not feel threatened by you. If you develop a reputation for nastiness, it will bite you in the ass. Those around you might turn on you to save their own skins, fearing that they will be next. Keep them from developing this mindset.

---

[101] As an example, I like to mention what happened during the Battle of the Wilderness to the Union army and how general Grant reacted. In a nutshell, they got mauled pretty badly. Things went from bad to worse with each bit of news from the front, but Grant kept it cool throughout — only succumbing to emotion privately at the end of the day.

Strategy 6: Never appear too perfect

This final strategy is designed to minimize the amount of resistance and resentment that you will face in any organization. By pursuing the techniques and strategies of control that apply both to other people and to organizations as a whole, you will acquire a lot of personal power and authority. Along the way, you will inevitably make some enemies. It's just going to happen. However, to at least avoid making too many of them, you can employ the strategy of never appearing too perfect. It works in tandem with never upstaging your boss and never show-boating.

Some enemies can't be helped. People will always feel envy and a bit of hatred for those who manage to outdo them. However, there are those whose hostility can be mitigated. By simply displaying some minor flaw, handicap, or issue that you have, it will give them the illusion that they are better than you — when you reveal it. This will boost their pride, sense of self-worth, and might even engender some sympathy (which can then be exploited at an appropriate time).

In terms of what form this weakness should take, that is entirely up to you. Just keep in mind that it shouldn't be something so horrible that it would cause damage to your reputation. If anything, it should bolster it because you are overcoming it. You might already have one naturally. You might be hard of hearing or have bad eyesight. You might be clumsy and uncoordinated. You might be a recovering alcoholic, a reckless driver, have ADHD, etc. If you don't have any natural minor flaws, acquire one. Another alternative is to make a simple (yet easily correctable) mistake from time to time. Don't make too many and/or any with disastrous consequences, but small mistakes can be made nonetheless.

Moreover, take ownership of your mistakes or flaws,

and openly admit responsibility — if you fix them yourself, great; if someone else finds one and corrects it, even better. Either way, people should know that you flubbed every once in a while. By showing that you are just as flawed as those around you, you can retain a bit of camouflage as you go about your plans.

Chapter 18
Corruption

The ultimate goal of toxick magick is the unraveling of the traditional centers of power and influence. This process of disintegration is done with the intention of clearing the current playing field of those who have wielded control over this planet for far too long with no other intention than benefiting themselves and their associates. These nexi of wealth and dominion need to be targeted for destruction, allowing humanity to reshape its future self. Once identified, action can be taken by the toxick magician to bring them down.

Within any large system that you choose to target (a corporation, political body, or social club), you will readily find the seeds of its future destruction. The germination and proper management of these maturing seeds can be exploited to maximize your control of whatever environment you find yourself living in. With this control, you can choose to bring about the destruction of the organization or group that you have chosen to infiltrate, or you can use it to direct positive change in the direction you wish to see.

Targeting

In our world, there is ultimately one nexus of control. This nexus is made of transnational corporations and the set of national and international political bodies that they favor. The transnational corporations wield control through the power of wealth, obtained through the exploitation of people and natural resources. The political bodies wield control through a near monopoly on brute force which also allows them to exploit the masses. Both of them are interconnected with individuals moving seamlessly between them.

In America, where I live, this nexus of control has classically been called "the military-industrial complex", or more accurately "the military-industrial-congressional complex." This system embodies the easily identifiable phenomenon of powerful individuals moving from government to business and vice versa as previously mentioned. They circulate through the "halls of power," accumulating wealth and influence. It is paralleled in other nations as well.

Fortunately, for our purposes, this is not a closed system. That is not to say that it is entirely open either. While entry is possible, much of what can currently be considered the "top echelons" are oftentimes populated by those who have inherited their access. They often intermarry and pass on what they possess to their offspring, thus giving them a great advantage over outsiders. Despite this, penetration is possible, even if the upper layers of authority remain out of reach. Note, it is not necessary to sit at the top of a hierarchy to bring it tumbling down.

The avenues of ingress for this system are via political parties (possible even within a single party state), the military (specifically through the officer corps), and the aforementioned transnational corporations (most effectively through the banking, financing, or energy sectors). One of these should be selected, researched, and then breached. Once this is accomplished, they can be harmed via the mechanisms below

Stagnation & Reaction

Both people and groups are constantly at risk of falling into predictable patterns. This should be cultivated. Never push for reform; always strive to maintain the status quo. In extreme cases, be an agent of reaction, always seeking to "return to our roots and first principles." Viable groups evolve, grow, and renew themselves periodically. This must be worked against. By harping on tradition and doing things "the way they have always been done," you can thwart efforts to breathe new life into a group.

This is particularly easy in larger and older organizations. Smaller groups tend to be nimbler and more responsive, while newer ones have yet to lay down any set foundational modes of action and are therefore receptive to change. Large organizations are exceptionally vulnerable in this regard. Constantly afraid of defection or schisms which might develop from changing things too abruptly, they are slow to adapt and respond. It's hard to keep any large group of people in constant agreement; in fact, it's impossible. So, they tend to be afraid of evolving. This conservatism should be constantly reinforced. In terms of older groups, they have been doing many of the same things the same way for a very long time. Keep those within these organizations imprisoned in the mindset that the old way is the best way. It worked in the past, it should now and in the future. Why risk failure by changing?

Of course, it's understood that change is both unavoidable and necessary for growth, and so many will advocate for it. When confronted with such people, remember that, deep down, human beings actually FEAR change[102], and fear is a powerful motivator. Remember to subtly play on that fear to keep those of a progressive and risk-taking mindset from pushing the larger body to reform. If change can't be avoided, attempt to ensure that it's reactionary rather than progressive: getting back to what the group's founders originally intended, returning to the original meaning or first principles, etc. Obstruct

---

[102] Humanity's instinctual fear of change is rooted in the need for food certainty and survival. If the rains don't come (change) then the crops won't grow and we starve; if the salmon don't run, or the herd of prey doesn't migrate into our territory, etc., we starve.

reform and you guarantee, in the long term, destruction. In the short term, you manufacture paralysis.

Paralysis

Nothing in this world is more vulnerable than the animal frozen in fear. It's ceased to be a moving target. It can be captured or slain with relative ease. Control over it is absolute; its fate is in your hands. What is true of animals is also true of humans and groups of humans. If a person or group of people is paralyzed, they have ceased to be a threat or risk; they can be controlled. This is started by promoting stagnation and completed by inducing paralysis. This is facilitated through the amplification of bureaucracy, the creation of needless complexity, and the proliferation of choices.

Nothing slows a person or a group to a crawl like bureaucracy. What should be straightforward, easy, and quick becomes convoluted, complicated, and slow. So, employ bureaucracy whenever possible. If it doesn't exist within the group, invent it. If it already exists, utilize it. More than that, work to proliferate the number of steps taken to accomplish any task. Add layers of approvals, forms to be filled out, validations to be done, rules to be checked, fees to be paid, hoops to be jumped through, every T crossed and every I dotted. If the amount of effort necessary to do something is too onerous and the cost of doing nothing cheap enough, most people will opt to do nothing. Bureaucracy, used correctly, puts the necessary barriers in place to keep things stationary.

Another alternative is the creation of needless complexity, the informal cousin of bureaucracy. This takes the form of pointless requirements, superfluous steps in any process, and the creation of manufactured difficulties. The first is easily induced in religious, spiritual, or occult groups but can be found in other organizations as well.

Before doing any rite, ritual or task, require that only very specific tools or items are used, regardless of whether or not there are viable substitutes. Insist that things are always done in a specific order and the more steps you can insist upon, the better. Additionally, you can make things like memorization a requirement. Mandate only using a special (preferable dead) language in rites and rituals. Call for complex gestures and gesticulations; the possibilities are endless. In mundane organizations like a business, this boils down to insisting on using only certain vendors, parts manufacturers, software applications, and custom tools.

Finally, paralysis can be created via swamping people with too many choices. The human mind is easily overloaded when presented with more than three choices at a time. So if one wishes to expedite a decision, one presents only two choices — to prevent a quick response, one gives five or six options (or more) to any conundrum. Additionally, if the stakes for the decision are raised by inflating its importance and questioning the decision maker's ability, many people will often freeze up as you force them into a position of self-doubt. They will be terrified that they will make the wrong decision, and to avoid making a mistake, they will make no decision at all: the actual outcome that you were aiming for.

Fragmentation

Breaking up an otherwise cohesive group is done through subtly promoting fragmentation. This is accomplished by creating an atmosphere of mistrust and suspicion. Whether or not you want to engage in this process will depend on one factor: Will fragmenting the group rebound to your benefit? Generally speaking, in any group the answer is usually "yes" — specifically in the situation where mistrust and suspicion are rampant but you, paradoxically, have developed a reputation for trustworthiness. In this environment, the warring individuals and factions will frequently turn to you for advice and direction. Ultimately, it will be up to your discretion whether or not you maintain the most basic level of harmony to continue to have power and control within the group or whether you decide to extract whatever value remains in terms of people, resources, etc. and let the system collapse.

Frequently, groups will get to this stage entirely on their own through the ego conflicts of its constituent members. This is a situation that is easily taken advantage of; otherwise you will have to create said divisions, which can be done in a number of ways. If you have effectively journaled those around you, that information can be used to effectively fragment the group. People who have revealed things to you can be betrayed by conveying their private opinions, hatreds, and jealousies to others, specifically to those who the negative thoughts, feelings and opinions are about.

In doing so, you have to be careful that it's not traced back to you. Sometimes this is as easy as requesting that the recipient doesn't rat you out, but that can be risky, as you're leaving yourself vulnerable to their discretion. It's better, where possible, to arrange for it to come to the target either anonymously, or through a third party: someone you know will not reveal you to be the source. Of those two options, the anonymous delivery is the best if you are trying to conceal yourself as the point of origin.

Keeping your hands clean is key. I've seen individuals who were intentionally sewing dissent within a group suffer blowback from their actions. Eventually, the other people within the group realized that while they were never in open conflict with anyone else, they nonetheless appeared as a suspicious common factor in every dispute which came about. They had positioned themselves, rather cleverly, as the go-to person to confide in. However, they regularly shared what others thought was private, resulting in a dust-up. When the rest of the group put this together, it was that individual alone who was ostracized.

Extraction

When all the signs in an organization point towards its imminent demise, it's time to consider if there is anything of value to retain. These resources should be identified and secured. It doesn't matter if it's information, material goods, money, or people; if it's a resource that you might extract value from, you should attempt to take it with you as the group falls apart. Once that occurs, you should consider whether or not you wish to strike out on your own or join another system. Obviously, if the organization in question is a business, you should have your next job lined up before this one is inevitably lost. If the ship is sinking, you should be the first rat that leaves, not the last. Perhaps you acquired enough resources to create your own company. Maybe you networked successfully so that you have an "in" at another. If you have created a "team" of people that would be of value, make all efforts to bring them with you.

If the item you want to extract is information, then there are plenty of methods available today to take it with you. Gone are the days of endless shelves of paperwork—a range of portable electronic devices exist; copy what you need and go. Just don't get caught during the duplication process.

During the exit process, refrain from creating or participating in any drama. "Don't burn any bridges," as the old saying goes. Even if your experience within a group was not ideal, keep up the appearance of having a positive attitude to it. If you bad mouth and smack-talk former associates, no matter how much it may be deserved, the only thing someone listening will wonder is, ""What does this person (you) say about me when I'm not around?" — Avoid engendering that kind of sentiment in others. It will close them off and hamper your efforts to either get information or favors from them in future.

Collapse

If you had initially entered an organization, company, or group with the intention of bringing it down, the final stage of the process is collapse. If the targeted collection of people is paralyzed, fragmented, and/or completely stagnated, final destruction is fairly easy. This often involves the (anonymous) publication of all of the group's dirty laundry at once. Again, make every effort to ensure that you are not identified as the source. If you are singled out, there is a chance that they will simply ostracize and scapegoat you as the source of their systemic problems. Which, to be fair, you were either creating or exacerbating.

Avoiding the blame falling on you is paramount. It serves two purposes: first, it will damage any remaining group cohesion if everyone suspects everyone else of being responsible. Second, it will allow you to continue to hammer away at them without you personally suffering any negative consequences. If you have remained within the group, you should leverage your position to make sure the collapse is complete. If you are no longer a part of the group, you can continue to affect it through those with whom you have maintained a good relationship.

By appearing blameless, you are then free to join another body, if you so desire, to commence the process all over again. If you did all of the above correctly, you might even come with glowing recommendations from the very people you sabotaged and exploited: an ideal state of irony.

Conclusion

In this work I have laid out the techniques and practices necessary for an individual to assert control over themselves, and their immediate social and professional environments. In addition, I have indicated that the ultimate purpose of obtaining this control is not merely to achieve economic success, sexual satisfaction and revenge against one's adversaries but to use this disciplined physical, emotional and mental mindset for a higher purpose.

We live in a world dominated, and controlled, by a collection of large, rapacious, political and corporate entities who are destroying the very planet they are exploiting. Leading these monstrous and vile juggernauts of exploitation are a collection of sociopathic and venal oligarchs. Men and women who deliberately, and gleefully, strangle and poison the world to satisfy their own jaded psyches: Their lust for wealth, status, and privilege. They give no thought to consequences, or to the future (except to plan their own escape in the event that everything collapses). Their hegemony MUST be broken.

Direct confrontation, in my view, is futile. They have too much power, too much wealth, too many resources and are just too large to hit head on and defeat. But, as is often the case, there is weakness in their strength. By requiring institutions, organizations and supporting human capital to keep their dominion they have exposed themselves to ruin, and thus given us a path to their ultimate destruction.

In volume two of "Ill Thoughts, Ill Words and Ill Deeds" I will provide a comprehensive list of our adversaries and their current machinations. I will lay out in exhaustive detail the strategies and tactics required to bring them down. Every individual utilizing the practices of toxick magick will thus have available to them a range of possible targets to practice their skills upon. With the larger goal of doing nothing short of preventing the destruction of the only habitable ecosystem known to exist in the universe.

Bibliography

48 Laws of Power - Robert Greene

Art of War, The - Sun Tzu

Body Language Secrets - Don Steele

Chaos & Sorcery Nicholas Hall

Exploring the World of Lucid Dreaming - Stephen LaBerge

Ganesh Mantras: https://vedicfeed.com/powerful-ganesh-mantras/

Get Anyone to do Anything - David Lieberman

Liber Null & Psychonaut - Peter Carroll

Liber Kaos - Peter Carroll

Magick in Theory & Practice - Aleister Crowley

Mindworks - Anne Linden

Paradigmal Pirate, The - Joshua Wetzel

Prime Chaos - Phile Hine

Psychology of Persuasion, The - Kevin Hogan

Psychopath's Bible, The - Christopher Hyatt

Quantum Psychology - Robert A. Wilson

Stronglifts 5x5 Workout - Medhi online, https://stronglifts.com/5x5/

Trance - Dennis Weir

Joshua Wetzel

Recent Titles from Megalithica Books

The Elemental Magic Workbook 2ⁿᵈ Edition by Soror Velchanes

This pragmatic workbook offers a complete course in elemental magic and provides a solid foundation for future independent work. Throughout history, individuals from diverse backgrounds and preparations have harnessed the elemental forces for spiritual enrichment, life balance, practical magic, and more. Though many cultures developed similar (and also valuable) models, our primary emphasis will be on understanding and working with the elements from ancient Greek and Hermetic perspectives, with a chaos magic twist. ISBN: 978-1-912241-18-7 Price: £11.99, $17.50

SHE: Primal Meetings with the Dark Goddess by Storm Constantine & Andrew Collins

The Dark Goddess is unpredictable, dispassionate, cruel, and often deadly. She reflects our deepest desires, fears, hopes and expectations. In this fully-illustrated book, Storm Constantine and Andrew Collins have selected a fascinating range of 34 goddesses, including some who are not so well-known. The pathworkings to meet them and explore their realms will offer insight into these often-misunderstood deities. (This title is also available as a limited edition, numbered hardback.) ISBN: 978-1-912241-06-4 Price: £12.99, $18.99

Quantum Sorcery 3ʳᵈ Edition by Dave Smith

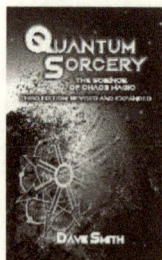

Quantum Sorcery is a modern magical system through which an individual can learn to manifest desired effects in the physical world through the exertion of Will, assisted by appropriate symbols and tools. This paradigm incorporates elements from earlier magical systems as well as physics, psychology, mathematics and biology to propose a mechanism by which such an act might occur through means more natural than supernatural.
ISBN: 978-1-912241-19-4 Price: £11.99, $17.50

www.immanion-press.com

196